LOVE IN ANCIENT GREECE

Leda and the Swan. Archaeological Museum. Venice. *Bettmann Archive*.

LOVE IN ANCIENT GREECE

by

ROBERT FLACELIÈRE

Translated from the French by
JAMES CLEUGH

CROWN PUBLISHERS, INC.
NEW YORK

First published in France in 1960 under the title
"L'Amour En Grèce" by Librairie Hachette

© *1962 by Crown Publishers, Inc.*
Library of Congress Catalog Card Number: 62-11804

PRINTED IN THE U.S.A.

Original French edition © *1960 Librairie Hachette*

CONTENTS

ILLUSTRATIONS

I

HOMER

*'We need not wonder (the kind elders said
when Helen paced the Trojan wall) that so
we suffer from her beauty. For it's made
one glance of hers worth more than all our woe.'*

RONSARD

IF we wished to study the ideas of love current among the Christians or the Muslims, we should have to start from a thorough knowledge of the Bible or the Koran. In the case of the ancient Greeks the first thing to do is to re-read Homer.

For the two Homeric epics, the *Iliad* and the *Odyssey*, though not, strictly speaking, sacred books, influenced Hellenic education and consequently the outlook of the Hellenes on the world, on life in general and love in particular, in a capital degree from the very beginning. The poems were used to teach children to read. The verses were learnt by heart and explained in the schools. At a later stage young people might hear the lines expounded by rhetoricians or philosophers. The citizens, throughout their lives, listened to recitations of the epics on such religious occasions as the Panathenea festival at Athens. Achilles, Hector and Ulysses thus became familiar friends and models among the people.

The rhetorician Heraclitus, who lived in the time of Augustus, states:

'At the most tender age innocent children making their first studies are weaned on Homer. One might almost say that as soon as we are out of long clothes our spirits draw in his verses like milk. He is ever at our sides as we grow up. In our youth he remains our daily companion. But it is in our maturity that we begin truly to appreciate him. We never tire of him even in old age. As soon as we have finished re-reading him we long to start all over again. It could plausibly be argued that only with life itself do our dealings with him cease.'

The Greeks in general considered Homer not only the prince of poets but also the greatest of theologians and moralists, though with this last estimate some of their philosophers did not agree. But as a rule his authority was judged supreme in questions concerned with science and conduct. He was regarded as the repository and interpreter of all wisdom, both human and divine, in a word, as the one expert on thought and life. His works were scrutinised in detail in order to discover the laws of religion, astronomy, physics, good manners and popularity. He was undoubtedly the 'schoolmaster of Greece', as even Plato (*Republic* 606 E) recognises, while deploring the fact.

In view of Homer's effect, accordingly, upon the intelligence and sensibility of the nation, it would be absurd to begin an enquiry into the Greek conception of love without first asking what importance was attributed to and what aspects were assumed by this sentiment, as old as humanity itself, in the *Iliad* and *Odyssey*.

It is certainly the case with the *Iliad*, as Aristophanes observed about the tragedy of the *Seven Against Thebes*, by Aeschylus, that it is a poem of war, 'full of Ares'. Nevertheless, love and the relations between the sexes play a far from negligible part in it.

In the first place the fascinating Helen, daughter of Leda and Tyndarus—or rather of Zeus himself—had been responsible, through her elopement with Paris, for the Trojan War and dominates both epics as a result of her 'divine' beauty. But we shall return to her later.

The Achaean chieftains of the *Iliad*, before leaving their country to follow Agamemnon and Menelaus to the Troad, generally had one legitimate wife in their palaces, together with one or more concubines, who were usually slaves.

Phoenix, who taught the young Achilles, relates in Book IX that he had been obliged as a youth to take refuge with Peleus, whose son, Achilles, he was eventually to educate. The old king Amyntor, father of Phoenix, had fallen in love with a young and beautiful girl, whom he intended to make his concubine and in whose favour he disdained his lawful wife, the mother of Phoenix. She thereupon persuaded her son to seduce the girl, 'so that she might come to loathe the old man', and the wife herself could then regain her influence. Phoenix obeyed his mother. But Amyntor found out what had happened, flew into a rage and cursed the boy, who shortly afterwards fled to take refuge with Peleus.

If a wife proved barren or gave birth only to daughters, the husband took steps to secure a male heir from a concubine, whom the wife, in such a case, was bound to tolerate. Menelaus, for instance, obtained a son, Megapenthes, in this way, his wife having presented him with a daughter only, named Hermione. Helen, as is well known, was by no means a model spouse. So she was hardly in a position to reproach her husband for his action.

But both wives and concubines stayed at home, like Penelope in Ithaca and Clytemnestra at Mycenae. Consequently, as the war lasted ten years, the chief Achaean warriors at any rate took care to obtain women 'to solace their ease'. There were many occasions on which they stormed and plundered cities, allied with Troy, in the islands or on the mainland of Asia Minor. Thence they carried off 'at the spear's point' fair captives, to serve them at table and often to share their beds.

Among the gifts promised by Agamemnon to Achilles in Book IX, if he would renounce his wrath and return to the battle, were 'seven women of Lesbos, skilled to perfection in their tasks'. Agamemnon adds that 'when Achilles himself had plundered the island, I took the women for my own share, deeming their beauty unequalled upon earth'. It is clear that the commander-in-chief of the camp before Troy did not stint himself of feminine company.

Each Greek leader had a favourite captive, with whom he slept. Book I of the *Iliad* mentions that Agamemnon's mistress was Chryseis, while Briseis was the concubine of Achilles. When Chryses, who was a priest of Apollo, came to beg Agamemnon to return his daughter, the king at first harshly repulsed him. 'I shall not give thee back thy daughter till she has grown old under my roof in Argos, far from her native land, working at her household tasks and sharing my bed.' Nor did Agamemnon hesitate to declare publicly on a later occasion: I 'prefer her to my wife Clytemnestra. For her beauty, her form, her understanding and her skill deserve it.'

When Calchas revealed that Apollo would not end the plague that was decimating the army until Agamemnon sent Chryseis back to her father, the 'king of kings', furious with Achilles, who had been supporting Calchas, sent two heralds to fetch away Briseis, as some compensation for the loss of Chryseis. Achilles did not object. He requested his friend Patroclus to hand Briseis over to the heralds and they brought the girl to Agamemnon. 'They departed along the line of ships,' says the poet, 'and the girl went with them reluctantly.' Homer is always discreet. He hardly mentions the feelings of Briseis. But her 'reluctance' seems to indicate that Achilles had won her affection, though he had slain her husband and her brothers at Lyrnessus.

In Book IX Agamemnon agrees to add 'the daughter of Brises, the girl I took away', to the seven Lesbians he intended to present to Achilles. He goes on: 'And I can swear to him a solemn oath that I never embraced her nor took her to my couch, as is nevertheless usual between man and woman.' Here the frank, in a sense innocent, recognition of the sexual impulse and the 'courtesy' of the Homeric heroes are alike notable. Agamemnon treated his fair captive with respect.

It is certain that the wrath of Achilles, which constitutes
the whole argument of the *Iliad*, cannot be ascribed to mere
vexation at being deprived of Briseis. His anger arose from
his public humiliation, the outrageous injustice inflicted upon
him, the best warrior in the army, by his unworthy commander. Whenever he broods upon this insult, his exaspera-
tion is embittered by reflecting that Agamemnon has carried
off and still retains one who was a 'spoil', bestowed upon
Achilles in 'honour', one whom he 'held as a gift from the
sons of the Achaeans'. Yet in Book IX he addresses Agamemnon's messengers as follows:

'Do the Atridae, alone among mortals, cherish their
consorts? All righteous and prudent men love and defend
the women they possess. Briseis was but a poor captive. Yet
I loved her from the bottom of my heart.'

Finally, in Book XIX, after Achilles and Agamemnon have
been reconciled through the death of Patroclus, the 'fair-
cheeked' Briseis is restored to Achilles. At this point Homer
allows her to speak for the first and last time, in a lament for
Patroclus.

'Friend, dearest to my heart when cruel fate overtook me,
thou wert living when I departed hence. Yet on the day of
my return I find thee dead. Evil after evil comes upon me.
I saw him who received me from my noble parents mangled
by the edge of bronze before my native city and my brothers
with him. . . . But on the very day when the swift-footed
Achilles slew my husband and plundered the city of godlike
Mynes thou didst bid me dry my tears and promised that
thou wouldst cause the godlike Achilles to take me for his
lawful wife, bringing me with his ships to Phthia, to marry
me among his Myrmidons. Therefore do I shed these many
tears upon thy corpse, my ever gentle friend.'

Briseis, like Andromache after the capture of Troy,
underwent the hard lot of war. But we have seen that
Achilles, who slaughtered her husband, was not uncongenial
to her. She even hoped to become his wife one day, in

Phthia, and Patroclus had gained her friendship by his good-natured and charitable promise to secure so brilliant a future. But the arrow of Paris, guided by Apollo, was to end her hopes with the life of Achilles himself.

His death is not recorded in the poem. Before it occurred the lovers lived together again for a certain period. In Book XXIV, after the touching and stately interview between Achilles and Priam, the hero and the king separate for the night, Priam to lie under the eaves of the tent and 'Achilles to sleep in the innermost apartment of his well-wrought dwelling, the fair Briseis beside him'.

The Achaeans before Troy could only dispose, for the time being, of captured women, though they hoped to augment the numbers of such prisoners after the town had fallen. Then not only the chieftains but also all the soldiers, even Thersites, would receive their share. Meanwhile the citizens, in spite of a siege which had now lasted nine years, led practically normal lives, with their wives and children, in the midst of what Albert Severyns calls a 'phoney war'.

In Book VI Hector leaves the field to return to Troy. 'The wives and daughters of the Trojan warriors who accompanied him immediately accosted Hector to ask after their brothers, sons, parents and husbands. But he told them all to address their questions to the gods. For many a grief already hovered over them. He came to Priam's splendid palace, its gates adorned with polished pillars. In one row of chambers slept the sons of Priam with their wives. Facing it on the other side of the courtyard stood the twelve chambers of Priam's daughters, in line. The rooms were wrought of square-hewn stone, with terraced roofs. In them lay the sons-in-law of the king, beside their gracious consorts.'

Priam had fifty sons and twelve married daughters, in addition to those unmarried. His chief wife Hecuba could of course only be the mother of a few of them. Lycaon, for instance, tells Achilles, in Book XXI, that he and his brother Polydorus were the sons of Priam and Laothea, daughter of

Altes, king of the Lelegae. 'For after Priam had added her to the number of his wives the daughter of Altes gave birth to Polydorus and myself.'

Priam was an oriental monarch and his harem seems to have been much more populous than those of the Achaean chieftains. No doubt Homer here introduces a touch of exotic 'local colour'. But in view of our previous reference to the concubines of the Greek leaders it is clear that the distinction was purely quantitative. In other respects Homer depicts the amorous sentiments of the Trojans as no different from those of the Achaeans. It is only in the *Odyssey* that he shows us a Greek husband and wife. But the conjugal affection between Hector and Andromache is already recorded in certain memorable scenes of the *Iliad*.

The first of these, in Book VI, is so well known that we need only quote a few lines. Andromache exclaims:

'Ill-fated husband of mine, thy valiant spirit will destroy thee! Thou hast no pity on thine infant son nor upon me, thy sorrowing wife, soon to be a widow. . . . Hector, for me thou art both father and dear mother, brother and young, vigorous husband. . . . Make not thy son an orphan and thy wife a widow!'

Hector answers: 'Ay, true enough. My soul and mind do know it. A day shall come when holy Troy, with Priam and all his people, must perish. . . . My heart is full of anguish for the future, yet not so much for the Trojans or even for Hecuba or Priam. . . . I fear above all for thee. Alas, could I but die and lie buried beneath a mound of earth, rather than hear thy cries upon the day when thou shalt be dragged into slavery!'

He then stretches out his arms to receive his son from the nurse.

'But the child turned away, hiding its face in the nurse's bosom and whimpering with fear at the sight of its father. The brazen armour and the helmet's plume were terrible to see. . . . The father and the revered mother laughed aloud.

Then glorious Hector straightway doffed his glittering helmet and placed it on the ground. He kissed the child and set it in the mother's arms. She, on receiving it upon her perfumed bosom, both wept and laughed. Her husband watched her with deep compassion.'

It has already been noted that the Homeric poems unquestionably had a great influence on ancient Greece. Consequently, this profoundly affecting scene must have stirred the readers of later ages, irrespective of the fact that the participants were Trojans. I have felt bound to recall the lines, celebrated as they are, for the very reason that the Greeks in general have no great reputation for conjugal fidelity and the kind of love known as 'Greek' in France is homosexual. Yet the Homeric poems are already a guarantee that matrimony in ancient Greece as elsewhere might be characterised by the tenderest and most natural of sentiments. Such love, too, is extended as a matter of course to the child, which is a pledge in concrete form of the physical and spiritual union of marriage.

Andromache reappears in Books XXII and XXIV, when she learns that her dreadful foreboding of Hector's death has come true, and when she weeps over her husband's body, uttering a heart-rending lament for her own fate and that of her son.

'How small is the child which we two, ill-starred parents, have brought forth! And yet my own lot will be even harder to bear. For thou, Hector, at the hour of death couldst not stretch, from the bed, thine arms towards me nor speak to me some word which, though I scarcely understood it, I should remember day and night with tears.'

Hecuba, Hector's mother, is also important in the *Iliad*. She is a model of conjugal and maternal affection. It is evident that she feels no jealousy of the numerous concubines of her royal husband and knows that she stands first in his estimation. In Book XXIV, when Priam prepares to leave for his bold visit to Achilles in the camp of the enemy, she acts as his confidential and loving attendant, advising him with as much wisdom as affection. Her maternal feelings for Hector are given poignant expression in Book VI, when she offers him wine in words full of tenderness, and above all in Books XXII and XXIV, when she begs him, from the rampart, to return to the city and escape the threats of Achilles, going so far as to bare her breast in the hope that he will listen to her, and again when she mourns over his corpse in overwhelming despair.

It is fair to say that, though the *Iliad* is indeed 'full of Ares', of acts of violence, abductions and murders, more gentle and humane sentiments, including those of the family and of lovers, are frequently and movingly described by a poet who must have experienced them himself.

The *Odyssey*, in which Ulysses returns home, also presents a picture of conjugal fidelity. But strictly speaking it is only the wife, Penelope, who remains faithful in every sense of the word, despite the importunities of her suitors. Ulysses himself, however, is faithful to her in spirit. For, although he becomes the lover of Circe and then for seven whole years lives with Calypso, he never forgets Ithaca and Penelope, to whom his heart is entirely devoted, if not his senses. He had already declared, for instance, in Book II of the *Iliad*, that 'he who is kept at sea even a month away from his wife frets aboard his well-wrought ship'.

Circe and Calypso, moreover, were not ordinary women. They were goddesses, witches who did what they pleased with the victims of their charms. Circe could actually change men into swine. There was thus every excuse for Ulysses. Agamemnon, as we have seen, made no secret of preferring his captive, Chryseis, to his wife Clytemnestra. The latter revenged herself terribly upon him for that insult and others which he offered her. But Ulysses only paid involuntary, if prolonged, visits to Circe and Calypso. He considered them far inferior to the 'wife of his youth', though she had neither their wealth, their power nor their personal attractions.

If the *Odyssey* in fact contains any 'moral' in this connection, it may well be expressed in the lines of Book VI
given to Ulysses, in which he wishes Nausicaa a happy
marriage. 'There is nothing better,' he tells her, 'or more
precious, than the perfect sympathy between husband and
wife at the domestic hearth. In it the jealous are confounded,
the friends of the family delighted and the couple themselves
at the pinnacle of happiness.'

But happy couples, people say, have no history. If so, the
case of Ulysses and Penelope was an exception. For their ten
years' separation due to the war was followed by yet another
such period of ten years. Twenty years is a long time, the
poet observes, in our brief human lives. For 'mortals on earth
are fugitive as leaves. The wind flings many to the ground.
But the thriving forest, when spring returns, grows many
more. Thus do the generations of mankind succeed one
another'. (*Il.*, Bk.VI). When Ulysses left for Troy his son
Telemachus was still a baby. But he had grown to a man and
a valiant warrior when he saw his father again. Ulysses and
Penelope had lost many of the years they might have spent
together. But absence itself sustains true love.

It is no exaggeration to say that the *Odyssey* is a romantic
variety of epic, the authentic forerunner of the novels of the
Hellenistic and Roman periods, in which lovers are long
kept apart by fate, subjected to painful and apparently endless ordeals and yet finally reunited to reap the reward, so
often postponed, so well deserved, of their almost superhuman mutual devotion.

In Book V Calypso tries to detain Ulysses by pointing out
her own merits. She even promises to make him a god if only
he will consent to remain with her, 'however much he may
long, day after day, to see his wife again'. She adds: 'Yet I
may claim that I am in no wise inferior to her in looks and
grace. Nor did I ever see a woman who could rival a goddess
in face or form.'

But the resolute, patient and wise hero replies:

'Revered goddess, hear me and pardon. I know well that, prudent as Penelope may be, compared with thee she is neither great nor fair. She is but a mortal and thou wilt never age nor die. . . . And yet the only desire I have each day is to come again into mine own, to see the hour, in my own house, of my return.'

During the voyage home his ship is wrecked in a storm. He swims ashore to the island of the Phaeacians, where he meets, in Book VI, the charming Nausicaa, daughter of the king. She has come with her attendants to wash linen garments at the mouth of a river. For in the Homeric poems upper-class women and girls were not confined, as they were to be at Athens, in special apartments. No one who has read the ensuing scene will ever forget it. The presence of mind and the good nature of Nausicaa enable Ulysses to clothe himself and visit the palace of Alcinous.

As the girl had shrewdly advised him, he at once throws himself at the feet of Arete, wife of Alcinous and mother of Nausicaa. For it was the queen who would be likely to pity him most and Nausicaa knew that her father could refuse her mother nothing. Thus we are here confronted with another model couple, like Hector and Andromache. But it is rather unfortunate for moralists that the bard Demodocus, when called upon to entertain the guests in the great hall, recites the improper tale of the adulterous intercourse of Ares and Aphrodite, to which we shall return. We may hope, perhaps, that this episode is an interpolation!

After the slaying of the suitors in Book XXIII there is an interview between Ulysses and his wife. The prudent Penelope still suspects that her husband, whose appearance has altered in the last twenty years, may be an impostor. She orders Euryclea to prepare the matrimonial couch, pretending that it is a movable article of furniture. But Ulysses, on his marriage, had used an olive-tree rooted in the soil to construct the bedstead, after which he had built the apartment round it. He is astonished at his wife's words. She of all people has succeeded in deceiving the famous trickster. He exclaims: 'Wife, is it from thy lips that I hear this painful news? Who could have removed my bed? 'Twould be impossible for the most cunning hand to do so without the aid of a god.'

Penelope replies:

'Pardon me, Ulysses. I knew thee ever for the wisest of men. The gods have loaded us with misfortune in denying us the pleasures of youth and of growing old together. . . . But forgive me this day and bear me no grudge for withholding welcome from thee at first sight. For deep in my heart I never ceased to fear that some man might cheat me with a false tale, since many are those wretches who think only to defraud. . . . But thou hast convinced me with irrefutable proof. Our bed is such as you have described. None knows it save us two and Actoris my maid. . . . Thou seest that, though my heart may have hardened, it now yields to thee.'

The next episode is also worth recalling.

'But Ulysses, when he heard these words, was seized with keen desire to weep. Sobbing, he held in his arms the faithful wife of his heart.' As for Penelope, 'the sight of her husband seemed as sweet to her' as that of land to shipwrecked men who have narrowly escaped death and come ashore. 'Her white arms could not leave their hold upon his neck.'

Eventually a female attendant, bearing a torch, 'led them to their chamber and returned to the hall, leaving them to enjoy the rediscovery of their couch and the rights to which it had once entitled them'.

So ends the *Odyssey*. For the rest of Book XXIII and the whole of Book XXIV are clearly later additions. The poem therefore really seems to have been composed, in essence, as a celebration of conjugal fidelity and happiness.

Such is Homer's view of human love. In the *Odyssey* he chose to tell an edifying tale. But he does not ignore the infidelity of Helen and many other women. He also knows that, although Ulysses was greeted on his return to Ithaca by the affection of the chaste Penelope, Agamemnon was murdered in his bath by Clytemnestra, who had become the mistress of Aegisthus.

In both poems the two worlds of gods and men are closely mingled. The gods of Olympus keep a sharp eye on earthly events and are fond of taking part in them, while the bards, on their side, know all about the proceedings, even the most secret, on Olympus. Later philosophers were scandalised by the behaviour of these deities, who resembled human beings in all their feelings but were stronger, taller, handsomer, more powerful and immune to death. Accordingly, if we wish to understand the whole of Homer's conception of love, we must take a look at the Olympians.

The first point to be noticed is that the divinities were on the whole much more uninhibited and promiscuous in their love affairs than mankind. The only two exceptions were the virgin goddesses Athena and Artemis.

But neither men nor gods, in Homer, are addicted to the homosexuality which later poets were to attribute to them. It is true that in Book XX of the *Iliad* there is a reference to Ganymede, 'who might have been taken for a god, being the fairest of mortals. Such was, indeed, the reason why the gods carried him up to heaven, that he might serve Zeus as cup-bearer and live among the blessed immortals'. But for Homer Ganymede is a cup-bearer and nothing more, not the minion of Zeus.

The latter married his sister Hera, who then became the goddess of matrimony. One might therefore have supposed that the divine pair would illustrate what I have called the 'moral' of the *Odyssey*. But this was far from being the case. Instead of the 'perfect sympathy' mentioned by Ulysses to Nausicaa, the household of the king and queen of the gods displayed scene after scene of wrangling and squabbling, out-and-out quarrels and even the exchange of blows.

As early as Book I of the *Iliad* Zeus had no sooner heard the prayer of Thetis to avenge upon the Greeks the humiliation by Agamemnon of her son Achilles than he exclaims: 'Trouble again! Thou, with Hera, art bringing me to strife. She will come to insult and vex me, as she does continually among the Immortals. Now once more she seeks to force dispute upon me, charging me with favouring the Trojans in this war. Be off at once, I say, for she might see you!'

The supreme ruler of gods and men had little authority in his own household, though the bending of his brows made Olympus tremble. He foresaw that Hera would soon hear of the request of Thetis. And, sure enough, as soon as the gods assemble, Hera starts a regular family row with him. To keep her quiet, he is obliged to use 'striking' arguments, threats of physical violence. Luckily the lame god Hephaestus succeeds in calming down the contestants, even diverting Hera herself, who is his mother, as well as all the Immortals. At last, as they watch him, they break into inextinguishable, truly 'Homeric' laughter.

Both Hera and Athena are on the side of the Achaeans. For neither goddess has forgotten the insult offered to them by the Trojan Paris, when he gave the prize for beauty to Aphrodite. Zeus, on the other hand, to please Thetis, tries to arrange for victory to go to Hector and his men, so long as Agamemnon refuses satisfaction to Achilles for the affront already mentioned. But Hera, very much a woman as well as goddess, employs typically feminine wiles in the astonishing episode known as 'Zeus Ridiculed' of Book XIV, whereby her husband's attention is diverted from Troy long enough to allow the Achaeans to rally.

After anointing herself with oil and ambrosia, combing her hair and donning her best clothes and ornaments, she goes to see Aphrodite. Her intention is to borrow—for women who have no reason for mutual affection often render each other such small services—the magic girdle, 'full of witchcraft' and capable of imparting sexual passion, which Aphrodite wears on her bosom. In order to obtain the loan of this article Hera tells an entirely imaginary story. She declares that she wishes to use the girdle for reconciling Ocean and Tethys, an old married couple who have fallen out. 'For long each has refused the bed of love to the other, so deeply has anger imbued their minds.'

Aphrodite, whether she believes this tale or not, lends Hera the girdle. The latter then obtains a promise from the god of sleep to make Zeus drowsy at a given moment. Next, in all her finery, she pays a visit to the summit of Mount Gargarus, from which her husband keeps a watch on Troy. She cunningly informs him that she has only come for a moment to ask his permission, like the good, obedient wife she is, to go and see Ocean and Tethys. For she tells him the same lie as she has told Aphrodite.

But her beauty, reinforced by the girdle's magic, renders Zeus ardent. He keeps her with him. 'For straightway love seized upon his prudent heart, a love as fervent as of old, on the day when they both for the first time lay together, without the knowledge of their parents.' From this passage we learn that the future goddess of matrimony had acted with some anticipation of the official ceremony. Zeus pleads with her.

'Hera, thou hast no need for haste. Come, let us to bed and taste the joys of love. Never hitherto has such strong desire for woman or even goddess penetrated my mind and subdued my heart, not even when I courted the wife of Ixion, who bore to me the valiant Pirithous, of godlike wisdom, or Danae of the well-turned ankles, the daughter of Acrisius and the mother of Perseus, most mighty of heroes, or her, Europa, who bore to me Minos and Rhadamanthus, or Alcmene or Theban Semele or Demeter, that rich-haired queen, or the renowned Leto, or even thee thyself. Far stronger is the love I feel for thee today, with such sweet passion is my spirit filled!'

The early critic Aristarchus already notes that this catalogue of mistresses is very much out of place here and more likely to offend than to attract Hera. But, interpolation or not, the passage certainly provides us with a long and instructive list of Zeus's infidelities.

This time, however, on Mount Gargarus, Hera wins the day, though in somewhat farcical fashion. For she coquettishly resists her husband in order to whet his appetite. 'Must we,' she asks, 'make a public show of ourselves in this conspicuous place? What if one of the Immortals should catch sight of us reposing here and go to tell all the other gods? Hast thou not thine own apartment, the work of thy son Hephaestus? Come, let us depart thither, since I see well that thy heart is set upon a couch.'

Zeus, however, will brook no delay. He envelopes them both 'in a great golden cloud', to hide their transports. Then he takes Hera in his arms.

'Beneath them the holy earth brought forth soft grass, rife with crocus, hyacinth and the lotus bloom, a thick and fragrant carpet upholding the twain in upper air. There did they lie . . . and thus slept Father Zeus upon the peak of Mount Gargarus, subdued by sleep and love, his wife in his embrace.'

Meanwhile the Achaeans, profiting by this respite from Zeus's control, launched a counter-offensive which re-established the situation in their favour. When Zeus, in Book XV, awakes and finds that his wife has tricked him, he loses his temper. A new matrimonial quarrel breaks out, even more violent than those which preceded it.

It is clear that Homer enjoyed the joke as much as we do. He obviously knew all about feminine coquetry and wiles. The cream of the jest is that he ascribes them to Hera, the goddess of marriage. The licence the Greeks allowed themselves in dealing with their divinities never ceases to surprise the modern reader. When Aristophanes, in the *Frogs*, renders Dionysus, who was actually the god of the theatre, so contemptible and ludicrous on the stage, he is scarcely more bold than Homer in his descriptions of the private life of the king of all the gods.

Two other Olympians come off very badly in the *Iliad*. Ares, the god of war, is depicted as a stupid and bloodthirsty brute. Aphrodite, the goddess of love, acts like a shameless and cowardly procuress. In Book V both these divinities, who are on the side of the Trojans, are wounded by a mere mortal, the hero Diomed, though it is true that the latter is aided by Athena, the daughter of Zeus. In the *Odyssey* Athena also becomes the patroness and inspiration of Ulysses.

Ares and Aphrodite figure together in the narrative recited by the bard Demodocus in the palace of Alcinous. It is often argued that this episode, in Book VIII of the *Odyssey*, was interpolated. But personally I can see no reason why the composer of the incident in which Zeus is 'ridiculed' should not have written that in which Ares and Aphrodite make love, which is recounted in the same boldly light-hearted manner.

Aphrodite's husband is Hephaestus, the lame smith. But she prefers the handsome fool Ares and receives him secretly in her matrimonial chamber. Hephaestus hears of her faithlessness from the Sun, who sees all 'and had detected them in the very act of love'. The skilled smith thereupon 'forged a net of unbreakable fetters to entrap the lovers'. He made the snare invisible, set it in position and feigned to go on a journey to Lemnos. Ares immediately accosted his mistress with the words; 'Haste, my dear one! To bed! Love shall give us pleasure! Hephaestus has gone away. By now he should be at Lemnos, among his Sintians, who speak a barbarous tongue.'

But the lovers were hardly bedded before they found themselves fast in the net constructed by the deceived husband. The latter instantly returned to Olympus and summoned all the gods, headed by Zeus, to see the offenders caught in the trap. The male gods at once assembled. But the goddesses, 'with the modesty suitable to their sex, remained at home'. Zeus, Poseidon, Apollo, Hermes and the rest broke into fresh 'Homeric' laughter and drew the following 'moral' from this scandalous situation: 'Good fortune attends not evil ways. . . . The cripple defeats the rake! The bandy-legged Hephaestus captures Ares! The price of adultery must be paid.'

The licentious character of this scene is still further stressed by the sly comments of Apollo and Hermes. The former remarks: 'Hermes, I believe that thou wouldst willingly endure such a load of chains, couldst thou but share the bed of golden Aphrodite!'

Hermes retorts: 'Would to heaven I could, far-shooting lord! Let me be loaded, Apollo, with thrice the weight of such chains without end, and come ye all to behold me, both gods and goddesses, so I might but sleep in the embrace of golden Aphrodite!'

The expression of this fervent wish was greeted by new bursts of laughter.

In Book XVIII of the *Iliad* Hephaestus is no longer married to Aphrodite but to Charis, one of the Graces, who seems to have made him a loyal and excellent housewife. The reception of Thetis by the couple presents an agreeable picture of something very like 'middle-class' behaviour. Hephaestus certainly deserved a peaceful settlement of his matrimonial troubles.

When divinities, in the *Iliad*, are wounded, it is not a serious matter. They feel a certain amount of pain. But they are soon cured. They are in no danger. For they are immortal. In the same way their love affairs cost them nothing and do not last, since deities have more liberty than mankind and are not doomed to perish. Aphrodite, like Clytemnestra, is an adulteress. But the poet speaks of these two personages in very different terms. Their adulteries, too, involve very different consequences. The deceived husband Hephaestus is merely made ridiculous and pays the lovers out. But Agamemnon is 'bled like a pig' (see Book XI of the *Odyssey*) by his faithless spouse. Death changes all. It gives weight and duration to human destiny, above all to human love. Among the Immortals love is merely a kind of game, without serious after-effects. But among men it is always an important, sometimes a tragic business.

There is no better proof of this statement than the career of Helen of Sparta. Her very name symbolises and sums up, in Homer, all the longing of mankind for some supreme beauty, that longing which the Greeks called *eros*.

She figures in both epics. The Trojan War originated in her abduction by Paris. Her responsibility is made clear as early as Book II of the *Iliad*, when the aged Nestor exhorts the Achaeans to capture Troy, so that 'each of us, through the possession of a Trojan woman, may exact vengeance, at long last, for all the fear and the weeping that Helen caused.'

In Book III Helen ascends the ramparts to view the strange duel on her behalf between her first and second husbands, Menelaus and Paris. She passes Priam and the Trojan elders, who admire her beauty and comment:

'It is no shame for the well-greaved Achaeans and the Trojans to suffer so long for such a woman. How wonderfully doth she resemble, to the eye, the goddesses of heaven! Yet, fair as she is, would she but take ship and leave this land, nor stay to be a scourge to us and to our sons!'

Ronsard's fine sonnet, inspired by this passage, is well known.

But Helen was aware of her guilt. She exclaims to Priam: 'Why did I not choose to die an evil death rather than follow your son hither, abandoning my house, my parents, my beloved daughter and my gentle women friends? Yet I did not die. And now I waste away in tears. . . .'

Nevertheless, when at the end of the same Book Paris is defeated and Aphrodite herself visits Helen to persuade her to console him and play her part of 'solacing the warrior', she eventually, after at first resisting the imperious demands of the goddess, yields to them. In the same way she begins, as soon as she confronts Paris, by bitterly reproaching him for his cowardice. Then she suddenly changes her tone, addressing him in kinder terms.

'Thou hast fled from the battle. Why didst thou not fall and die beneath the blows of my first husband, that mighty hero? I have heard thee boast—deny it not!—that thou wouldst conquer Menelaus, the beloved of Ares. . . . Come, challenge him a second time, face him in the forefront of the fight! . . . Yet, no, insist not on it, I myself beg of you. Never again provoke the fair-haired Menelaus to combat in thy folly, lest he instantly despatch thee by the spear.'

She had originally spoken 'with her eyes turned from him', in Homer's finely imagined phrase. Racine noted in his own copy of the *Iliad*, against this line: 'Helen turns her eyes away from Paris because she wishes to scold him and she knows well that her love for him will return if she looks upon him.' This change occurs, in fact, as soon as she pronounces the words: 'Yet, no, insist not. . . .' It is a highly characteristic alteration of mood. Helen continually oscillates between repentance and love, like so many other men and women torn by the opposition of duty and passion. But in her case Aphrodite at last wins the day. 'On hearing these words,' writes the poet, 'he turned straightway towards the couch and his wife followed him.'

Thus Helen's affections were divided. She retained 'a gentle glow of love for her first husband, her parents and her city'. She bitterly regretted her immoral action. But Paris was Paris. Faint-hearted he might be. But how handsome and desirable he was!

She respected her brother-in-law Hector far more, not hesitating to proclaim the fact while both men were present. In Book VI Hector returns to the city in search of Paris, who has been much too long 'on leave' with his wife. She tells Hector:

'Brother-in-law, I am no better than a froward bitch, detested by all. Would that, on the day of my birth, I had been seized and carried off by some ill wind of storm to a mountain peak or the echoing waves of rolling seas. There would I have been drowned for ever, without having caused so much evil. But since the gods have brought these woes to pass, I might at least have had a more worthy companion, one who could feel indignation and resent an insult. This man is not, nor ever will be, resolute in mind. A day will come when he will pluck the fruit of his weakness. But no more of this. Enter, brother-in-law, and seat yourself. Thou above all art tormented by the cares of which we are the cause, both I, bitch that I am, and Paris through his deed of shame. Dread is the fate that Zeus has made us bear, that men may sing of it in distant ages.'

She knew that she would be famous for ever. If she had been made the wife, like Andromache, of the gallant hero Hector, would she have thus continued to regret her first husband? We cannot be sure. But in any case, in Book XXIV, she mourned sincerely for Hector, praising the good nature and delicacy of which he had always given proof where she was concerned.

'Hector, thou wast the dearest by far to me of all my brothers-in-law. . . . 'Tis twenty years since first I came from overseas and in all that time thou didst never speak a harsh or cruel word to me. . . . Whenever anyone in the palace cast reproach upon me, thou didst defend me. I grieve therefore, from a broken heart, as much for my own misfortune as for thine. Henceforth there will be none to show me courtesy or kindness on the broad plain of Troy, where all do hold me in abhorrence.'

We are here reminded of the lament of Briseis over the body of Patroclus. Helen admires Hector for his courage and honesty. She is touched by his indulgence. Though physically, through the will of Aphrodite, she is enslaved by Paris, it is Hector whom her mind prefers. It is clear therefore that in the Homeric world the virtues of fortitude and compassion typical of the true 'knight' commanded deep respect and affection, even between man and woman, quite apart from any element of passion. This sentiment, that of friendship, called *philia* by the Greeks, was often regarded by them as superior even to *eros*. The most striking example of *philia* is the impassioned friendship, but in the Homeric poems uncontaminated by desire, felt by Achilles for Patroclus.

When Helen reappears in Book IV of the *Odyssey*, she has resumed her position at Sparta, in the palace and bed-chamber of Menelaus. She has lost nothing of her beauty and qualities of mind. She is the first to recognise Telemachus, from his likeness to his father.

As an accomplished housewife, when she sees Menelaus and his guests grow sad, she secretly mixes their wine with a drug which 'assuages grief and puts an end to weeping'. For she has some knowledge of magic and has brought back wondrous medicaments from Egypt. She is also a prophetess. For in Book XV she correctly interprets an omen as fore-casting the imminent return of Ulysses.

When Telemachus is about to leave Sparta she insists upon making him a personal gift, clearly recognisable as her own handiwork. It is an ample veil, which she has herself woven and embroidered.

'I too have a present to offer thee, dear child. Take and keep this my work in memory of me. When the day of marriage comes to heap joy upon desire, let thy wife wear it. But till then let thy mother hold it safe at home. Farewell. I pray that thou mayest return to thy tall house, in the land of thy forefathers.'

The Homeric Helen is conscience-stricken, almost a repentant sinner. Yet she is capable of blaming the interven-tion of Aphrodite for her own actions, justifying them, like other women, by declaring that she has been no more than the plaything of the goddess. For, as in Racine's line: *Venus in all her power hath fastened on her prey.*

The phrase aptly characterises the scene in Book III of the *Iliad*, when Helen rebels against the divine procuress before yielding to her threats. The Homeric heroes, however, remain free agents, despite the deprivations with which fate and the will of the gods afflict them. They proudly assume personal responsibility for all their actions. At the same time it appears possible that Helen herself considers the physical attraction that binds her to Paris a passion she cannot acknowledge, a torment which simultaneously shames and delights her and which she feels herself too weak to repel.

But this is not the essential point. Homer embellished a legend already current, in which beauty played the chief part. The Greeks continued for centuries to study this idea, as it was expressed in his two epics. Their innate appreciation of both bodily and moral beauty was kindled in this way to a blaze of enthusiasm. For they were unquestionably a people of exceptional sensibility and artistic refinement. They could never be indifferent either to the harmony of line and shape or to moral virtue, which they called *arete* or *to kalon*.

Book XXII of the *Iliad* contains a very curious passage in which the aged Priam foresees his death. He prophesies that after being killed by the Achaeans he will be devoured by his own dogs.

'When a young warrior falls, slashed by the sharp edge of bronze, in the battle, his aspect is not hateful to the eye. All that is visible of his body, though dead, remains handsome. But when the grey hairs, the white beard and the entrails of an aged man are mangled by dogs, what worse fate can befall wretched mortals?'

Such close attention to physical attractiveness, even that of a corpse, seems to be highly characteristic of the Greek mind. Invalids and the dying were in the habit of covering their faces to conceal the features which suffering had distorted. The flute, or rather the oboe, was often despised, as an instrument suitable only for slaves, on account of the inevitable swelling of the cheeks which accompanied the playing of it.

The language itself of a nation is a clue to its most commonly held ideas. In Greek the word *kalos* means both beautiful and noble, *aischros* both ugly and shameful. Beauty, accordingly, for a Greek, was the same thing as nobility, and ugliness a shameful thing. We shall return to this point. But it is of some importance to note that this basic conception of beauty as an indissoluble union of both physical and moral elements is already well attested in the Homeric poems.

Helen was supposed to be the daughter of Tyndarus. But her real father was Zeus. She was a goddess before being a woman and she became the personification of beauty. She figures comparatively seldom in the *Iliad* and *Odyssey*, but always significantly. The fascination of her presence may be said to dominate, at all events in the aesthetic sense, both epics.

A good example of the influence exercised by Homer in this connection and also of the permanence of the passion for beauty throughout the centuries of Greek antiquity is the *Praise of Helen* composed by the Athenian orator Isocrates in the fourth century B.C. The piece is at the same time a prose hymn to beauty itself.

'Helen shared the privileges of beauty, the most revered, precious and divine of boons. . . . Everything which lacks beauty is devoid of charm. . . . Virtue itself is only appreciated because it is the fairest habit of the mind. . . . When we have need of a thing, we simply want to possess it. But the impassioned longing for beauty, when it enters our hearts, has a power which exceeds the strength of the will with a degree of ease proportionate to the intensity of beauty's radiance. . . . The moment we perceive beautiful persons we feel well disposed to them. They and the gods are the sole beings whom we never cease to serve. We are more delighted by becoming their slaves than by issuing orders to others.'

The 'impassioned longing for beauty', according to legend, first instigated the Trojan War. Homer's choice of it as his subject is significant. His poems, from which Greek children learnt to read, gave them a foretaste of the immense power, for evil as for good, of those 'gifts of Aphrodite' which Paris, in Book III of the *Iliad*, defends to his brother Hector.

'Yet reproach me not for the beguiling gifts of golden Aphrodite. The shining gifts of the gods are not to be scorned, which they alone bestow upon us, which none could of his own will acquire.'

It may well be thought that beauty was regarded by the Greeks as a favour conferred by heaven, the most precious and yet also the most formidable they could receive.

Both Achaeans and Trojans, then, had concubines. Nevertheless, marriage was considered by both sides a respectable and venerable institution. Some Trojans, Priam for instance, were polygamous. But the Achaeans, the forefathers of the Greeks, never had more than one legitimate wife. Their descendants in the age of Pericles might also, like Agamemnon, possess concubines. But most of the citizens were monogamous.

In the highest ranks of Homeric society, the only ones of which we have any considerable knowledge, the father who wished to see a daughter married would call together a number of suitable young men of good family and invite them to compete for her hand. Those who agreed to do so would visit him, bringing with them victuals and all kinds of gifts. On such occasions feasts, entertainments and merry-making took place. In Book XVIII of the *Odyssey* Penelope observes:

'In order to please a girl of noble blood and much wealth men vie with one another in generosity. They entertain her parents at her house, conveying thither oxen, fat sheep and splendid presents.'

The father would then often arrange trials of strength among the suitors. For the widespread Greek fondness for athletics even affected the choice of a future husband. In legendary tales the father sometimes himself participates in the competitions, giving his daughter only to the youth who vanquishes him. The 'royal race' between Oenomaus and Pelops is an example. The archery contest to which Penelope subjects her wooers in Book XX of the *Odyssey* is a survival of such trials, designed to distinguish the most skilful, strong and courageous competitor, who would then deserve to marry the princess.

It was of course the girl's father, not herself, who selected the husband. The winner thereupon offered his host gifts of considerable value, constituting a kind of purchase price for the bride, who, in the Homeric phrase, 'was worth much cattle'. But the prospective father-in-law might also confer a dowry upon the pair, such as Agamemnon promises to Achilles in Book IX of the *Iliad* if the latter will consent to become his son-in-law.

'I have three daughters. . . . Let him take which of them he pleases to the house of Peleus without obligation to me. I myself will bestow rich marriage gifts upon the pair, such as a father never yet made to his daughter, presenting her with seven of my fine cities.'

On the day of the wedding the bride's father gives a great banquet. In the evening the new wife is solemnly conducted to her husband's house, by torchlight, seated in a chariot and surrounded by a festal escort, as represented by the god Hephaestus on the shield of Achilles, described in Book XVIII of the *Iliad*.

'He showed also two fine cities of men. In the first a joyous wedding train was proceeding, with bride and bridesman under escort, by torchlight, while spectators raised the nuptial chant. Many young dancers whirled to the sound of flutes and lyres. The neighbouring housewives, standing each upon her threshold, marvelled at the scene.'

As for family life, we have already seen something of it in the relations between Hector and Andromache, Ulysses and Penelope, Alcinous and Arete. One of its most striking features, very different from the customs of classical Greece to be examined in Chapter IV, was the comparatively unrestricted freedom of movement enjoyed by women. Hecuba, Andromache and all the Trojan ladies, not to mention Helen, strolled at will through the city, even upon the ramparts and among the warriors. Women of the upper classes were merely accompanied by at least one female attendant. This rule remained invariable in ancient Greece at all periods. The unmarried Nausicaa even left the city with her feminine companions, going to the beach, where she bathed and played at ball. Such a scene would be inconceivable in Periclean Attica.

It is true that the men took their meals unaccompanied by their womenfolk in the great hall, the *megaron*, of the palace, while the women ate in the apartments, the *gynecea*, reserved for their use. But as soon as the repast was finished, Penelope in Ithaca and Helen at Sparta joined the men. The former was actually on one occasion somewhat sharply rebuked by her son Telemachus, who was, of course, in his father's absence, the head of the family.

'Go, return to thy dwelling and resume thy labours at the loom and distaff. Talk is the affair of men, of myself, the master of this house, above all.' (*Od.* I, 356–9.)

In general, however, Penelope was treated with respect by all.

Arete, the wife of Alcinous, enjoyed very great prestige.

'Alcinous paid her more honour than is accorded now to any woman in the world who keeps house at the bidding of a husband. She was and yet is beloved and revered by her children, by the king Alcinous himself and by his subjects. In the street all eyes turned to her as to a god and words of greeting were spoken. Wise was her judgment, great her generosity. Disputes, even among men, were settled by her benevolence.' (*Od.* VII, 66–74.)

At the beginning of this passage the comparison made by the poet between the heroic age and his own perhaps suggests that in his personal opinion the situation of married women had changed noticeably for the worse since that time.

Between the epoch of the Mycenean or Achaean civilisation and that in which Homer lived great racial migrations had taken place. Greece had been gradually conquered by the Dorians and the age of bronze gave way to that of iron. It may have been the Dorians who introduced coarser manners and a different conception of society, in which men cultivated a peculiar ideal of uncompromising virility, despised the 'weaker sex' and kept to themselves, scarcely ever meeting their wives except in that 'unique social centre, the matrimonial bedchamber', as André Bonnard puts it in *Lettres d'Humanité*, V, 1946, p. 33. Such habits eventually created an atmosphere favourable to the rise and development of homosexuality.

It is important to note that no trace of this tendency, or of misogyny, is to be found in the Homeric poems. For the speech of the shade of Agamemnon in Book XI of the *Odyssey*, vv, 405–455, has no bearing on the latter sentiment. It was natural for him to remark, after being murdered by Clytemnestra, that 'there is no more faith in woman'.

2

MYTHOLOGY

' Great love brims the banks of death.'

PROPERTIUS.

IN the foregoing chapter we have confined our investiga-
tions to the deities and heroes who play their parts
directly upon the stage of the two Homeric epics. But in
addition to the tale of the wrath of Achilles, which is the
subject of the *Iliad*, and the story of the return of Ulysses, with
which the *Odyssey* deals, Homer alludes very frequently to
mythological personages, human and divine. His testimony
must therefore again be examined. But this time we shall
consider it in common with that of all the poets who
succeeded him, 'picking up crumbs from his table' and
inspiring in their turn certain great legends. These were
treated by Hesiod, then by the lyrists, of whom the most
eminent is Pindar, and finally by the dramatists Aeschylus,
Sophocles and Euripides.

Most of the ancient gods of Rome were mere abstractions,
summarily personified and given various functions. But the
abundant imagination and inventive spirit of Greece created
innumerable highly diversified narratives about gods and
heroes with contrasting and complex characters. This
immensely fertile garden of legend had both religious and
poetic significance. The Greeks believed in the existence of
the divine or superhuman beings they had conceived. They
sacrificed to such figures, worshipped them with ritual,
feared their wrath and hoped for their favour. Yet at the same
time the poets developed and often transformed the myths
they found in popular superstition, so that faith never
became fixed in the rigid framework of a creed or dogma.

Nor were such activities confined to literature. The plastic arts, especially sculpture and painting, illustrated legendary themes, thus not only rendering them more familiar but also sometimes modifying their ideas. Greek vase-painting, for example, constitutes a most attractive compendium of the national mythology.

Such legends survive even in modern times. Many contemporary writers, especially dramatists, take their subjects from Greek myths, which have preserved for centuries their wonderful symbolic and evocative powers.

In ancient Greece the literary and plastic works inspired by religious mythology expressed the spirit of the people at its deepest level, before it went on to create philosophy and history. It is therefore in such literature and visual art that we must look for clear definition of ancient Greek notions of love.

Of the deities, Aphrodite and her son Eros are those most essential for our purpose and we may for the time being neglect the rest.

Aphrodite's appearances in the *Iliad* and *Odyssey* do little to recommend her. She is presented as both an adulteress and a procuress. Let us see whether subsequent testimony may lead us to modify the portrait in some degree.

In Homer Aphrodite is the daughter of Zeus and Dione, an ancient goddess worshipped at Dodona. In Book V of the *Iliad*, when wounded by Diomed, she runs to her mother in tears, seeking consolation and caresses. But it is Hesiod who relates the most popular story about her. In the *Theogony* he describes how Cronos, son of the first parents, Ge (Earth) and Ouranos (Heaven), castrates his father with a billhook.

'He hurled the scrotum, severed by the steel, into the sea, where it drifted away. And all about it poured white foam from the divine organ.'

The Greek word for foam is *aphros*, whence the name Aphrodite is derived. But this etymology, like so many others, is clearly fanciful. The foam here is not that of the sea. It is the sperm of the mutilated god. Hesiod continues:

'Of this foam a girl was formed. She came first to Cythera,
then to the isle of Cyprus, where the fair and venerated
goddess stepped ashore.'

The most famous cults of Aphrodite were in fact practised
in Cyprus, so that Homer already calls her *Kypris*, the
Cypriot, and on the small island of Cythera, south of the
Peloponnese, off Laconia. The goddess, born of the waves
opposite Paphos in Cyprus, was also called *Anadyomene*, 'she
who arises', i.e. emerges from the surface of the sea. She was
represented in this attitude by Phidias on the pedestal of his
statue of Zeus in the temple at Olympia. She is being welcomed ashore by Eros, while Peitho (Seduction) crowns her,
and all the gods and goddesses contemplate her with intense
admiration. The centrepiece of the renowned Ludovisi
throne in the Termi Museum, Rome, probably shows her
rising from the waters and being received by the Hours, who
are draping her in a cloak. By reason of her birth Aphrodite
was destined to be not only the goddess of love but also a
marine deity invoked by sailors.

Hesiod was much more of a woman-hater than Euripides.
After reciting the birth of Aphrodite he immediately adds:
'Her gifts are the prattling of wenches, grins and trickeries,
as well as sweet pleasure, tenderness and good nature.' In
the *Works* he relates the celebrated myth of Pandora. She
was a beautiful young girl, fashioned by the gods, at Zeus's
command, to plague mankind, in the very image of Aphrodite. For that goddess, says Hesiod, 'lavished upon her grace
and dolorous desire, together with sore aching cares'. She
was also endowed with 'impudence and a crafty heart'. It is
clear, therefore, that Aphrodite's morals had not improved
since the days of Homer.

The origin of most of the Greek gods is obscure. But the
motherless Aphrodite, born of the sperm of Cronos, seems
likely to have come from Asia. The islands of Cyprus and
Cythera were probably her chief stages on the way to the
establishment of her cult in Greece. She may well have been

Aphrodite Rising from the Sea. Fourth-century relief. Ludovisi Throne. Termi Museum, Rome. *Bettmann Archive.*

the sister deity of the Mesopotamian Ishtar and the Phoenician Astarte, who presided over the propagation of the species and universal fecundity.

At Athens Aphrodite was particularly connected with gardens. Flowers, fruit and vegetables grew under her protection. At Thebes she was the mother of Harmonia, bride of the Phoenician Cadmus.

In Hesiod she is no longer the mistress but the lawful wife of Ares. For beauty belongs to supreme strength, which is that of the god of war. All the same, she has many lovers, both gods and heroes.

As a marine goddess, she becomes associated with Poseidon. As we have seen, she was at one time the fickle wife of Hephaestus. Her union with Hermes, the messenger-god—a pander, as she is a procuress—produced a being who partook of both sexes, the Hermaphrodite, later the subject of somewhat perverse fancies in the closing stage of Greek art. Dionysus, the god of wine and ecstasy, gave Aphrodite a son, Priapus, of a most unseemly character.

But Aphrodite's loves included men as well as gods. She conceived a passion for a handsome youth who was, like herself, of oriental origin. He was called both Adonis and Tammuz. Aphrodite went into deep mourning when he was killed out hunting. On Mount Ida in the Troad she had intercourse with Anchises and bore to him Aeneas. The legend is already known to the poet of the *Iliad* and the author of the *Hymn to Aphrodite*. Accordingly, when the myth of the Trojan ancestry of Rome took shape, Venus-Aphrodite could be regarded as the foundress of the Roman power itself.

As well as a sea and sky divinity, known as Urania in the latter capacity, Aphrodite was also *Pandemos*, 'she whom all adore', and consequently without doubt a city goddess. Apparently it was Socrates who first thought of contrasting Urania with Pandemos, the former symbolising pure, heavenly love and the latter personifying carnal, earthly passion. Among the Romans Aphrodite Pandemos developed into Venus Vulgivaga, a Venus of the cross-roads or the public street.

It is important to note that Aphrodite, like Ishtar at Babylon, was a chthonian, i.e. an 'infernal', goddess. This side of her legend recalls the perpetual association of love with death. At Argos and Delphi she was Epitumbia, the protectress of tombs. At Corinth she was named Melanis, the 'sombre'. Certain ceremonies of funereal type were performed in her honour. Sometimes she seems almost one with Persephone.

In consequence of the numerous murders caused by love, Aphrodite was also known as Androphonos, 'man-slayer'. According to Plutarch she was worshipped under that name in Thessaly, at a sanctuary where Lais, the famous courtesan, had been stoned to death by the women of that country. They had been jealous of her beauty. But she had not really deserved such treatment. For she had abandoned Corinth and her profession to retire with a single lover named Hippolochus.

Many of Aphrodite's victims, mostly women, are known by name. They included Helen, referred to in the previous chapter, and Medea, the witch of Colchis, who killed her father, her brother and finally her own children for love of Jason. Then there was Atalanta, the virgin who resisted marriage and could run so fast that one of her wooers was only able to beat her in the race through a trick suggested by Aphrodite, that of the golden apples. Hippodamia only succeeded in eloping with Pelops by causing her father's death and betraying Myrtilus, whose curse subsequently afflicted the whole House of the Atridae, who were descended from Pelops. Finally, the Cretan royal ladies Pasiphae, Ariadne and Phaedra underwent misfortunes which are well known from Racine's *Phèdre*.

Yet, in spite of Aphrodite's sombre and cruel traits, she remained the personification of feminine beauty and charm transferred to the world of heaven, as we have seen that Helen represented them on earth. On occasion Aphrodite is found as a goddess of marriage, like Hera. But she more often presides over sexual unions without stability. Her female attendants are the Hours, the Graces and Peitho. The gods Eros and Himerus (Desire) accompany her.

Her power is immense, literally global. She causes a 'world' war between Greeks and barbarians, as the ancients would have called it, viz. the Trojan War, with its long record of suffering and death. But her control even extends as far over the gods and the whole of nature as it does over humanity.

Of the tragedians Aeschylus, as we shall see, disdained Aphrodite, though not Eros. But all the other Athenian dramatists celebrated her omnipotence. 'Great is the force', declares Sophocles in the *Trachiniae*, 'to which Kypris owes her victory.' The statement is a far cry from the description in Book V of the *Iliad* of the same goddess in her enfeeblement and terror. Phaedra's nurse, in the *Hippolytus* of Euripides, affirms:

'Kypris is irresistible when she assaults with violence. The foe who yields is gently treated. But woe to any whom she finds arrogant and haughty. When she has once seized him, the torments she inflicts are known only to God, as Hippolytus will learn to his cost. She haunts the altitudes of heaven, frequents the waves of the sea and all life is born of her, Kypris. She sows its seed, she bestows love and we owe to her all the births of this world.'

Long before Lucretius wrote his Latin poem the Greeks recognised and extolled the all-embracing power of Aphrodite, mistress and source of all living things, whether vegetable, animal or human.

She inspired their artists no less than their poets. As regards sculpture, we have already mentioned one of the works of Phidias and the Ludovisi throne. This is not the place to catalogue the various types of statues of the goddess which are to be found in museums. She is represented at the bath, in gardens, partly clothed, in modest and crouching attitudes and so on. The greatest Greek sculptors, Alcamenes, Scopas and in particular Praxiteles, delighted, on the pretext of celebrating Aphrodite, in tirelessly reproducing the grace of the feminine form and enhancing it by the harmonious relation of line and mass, culminating in the mysterious Venus of Milo, a statue of which neither the creator nor the date are known.

In antiquity the most celebrated of these works was the Aphrodite of Cnidos by Praxiteles. Replicas have come down to us. Lucian describes it as follows in his *Erotes*.

'The statue is a flawless work of Parian marble. The goddess's lips are slightly parted in a disdainful, ironic smile. No garment veils her charms. But one hand screens her modesty with a casual gesture.'

Lucian goes on to relate a somewhat improper anecdote. A certain youth had fallen madly in love with this marble divinity, so much so that he shut himself up one night in the temple where the statue stood. 'I need not', Lucian continues, 'be so indiscreet as to recount the details of the crime that he committed on that disgraceful occasion. Signs that he had embraced the statue were visible at daybreak, in the shape of a stain upon the marble. After perpetrating this outrage the young man threw himself into the sea', of which it will be recalled that Aphrodite had been born.

The goddess is sometimes represented in reliefs or vase-paintings as riding a swan or a goat, these creatures symbolising her respectively as Urania and Pandemos.

When the Hellenistic age began in the fourth century images of Aphrodite were more and more often depicted on vases. For at that period the Greeks were increasingly developing a taste for voluptuous scenes. *Tryphe* (sensual luxury) was no longer considered a vice, but a praiseworthy ideal.

At the time of Pericles in the preceding century statues

Venus de Milo. The Louvre. *Andreas Feininger*.

Torso of Aphrodite. The Louvre. *Andreas Feininger*.

Aphrodite Riding a Swan. Drinking vessel. British Museum. *Histoire de l'Art dans L'Antique*, Perrat and Chipiez, Librairie Hachette, Paris.

of goddesses or women were nearly always clothed. Nudity was reserved for male figures. But in the fourth century fewer and fewer garments were represented on the female form. We may fairly deduce that this tendency indicated certain changes in morality and erotic sensibility. In any case, as we shall see, it was then that family life began to deteriorate morally, in Athens at any rate.

Like the other Olympians Aphrodite was worshipped with a special ritual in most of the Greek cities. But this was not the case with Eros. He was not one of the twelve chief gods of Olympus. Very few shrines were dedicated to him. In metropolitan Greece only one is known to have existed in early times. It was at Thespiae.

As the word *eros* was a common noun meaning simply 'love', the very name of Eros proves that the god was at first a pure abstraction of allegorical type, like Peitho and Himerus or Pothos, who also accompanied Aphrodite. Homer is not acquainted with Eros. But in Hesiod's *Theogony* he suddenly appears as a primitive deity. His birth is placed long before that of Aphrodite or any of the Olympians. He is said to have been born at the same time as the world itself, when only Chaos and Earth existed. Hesiod was a Boeotian, and it was in that region, at Thespiae, that Eros had long been worshipped in the form of a sacred stone. His festival, the Erotidaea, is referred to in Roman times by Plutarch, another Boeotian. Like the more important religious ceremonies of the Greek world, the Olympian, the Pythian and the Panathenaean, it took place every fifth year. It was celebrated at Thespiae with great splendour at the same time as that of the Muses, whose shrine stood at the foot of Mount Helicon near the city. The mutual relations of Eros and the Muses are obvious, for love has often inspired poets. Euripides notes that 'Eros makes poets even of yokels'.

Eros was a primitive deity not only for Hesiod but also in the Orphic cosmogony. Aristophanes, for example, writes in the *Birds:* 'In the beginning was Chaos, Night, black Erebus and broad Tartarus. But neither earth nor air nor sky existed. In the infinite womb of Erebus first black-winged Night laid a seedless egg'—the Cosmic Egg—'from which in due season arose Eros, the desired one, whose back sparkled with wings of gold and who raced like the wind. It was he who mingled with Chaos in broad Tartarus and brought forth our species', i.e. the birds.

Similar conceptions are often found in the lyric and tragic poets of the sixth and fifth centuries. In a fragment of the *Danaids*, by Aeschylus, Eros causes the sky and the earth to unite. Earth is fertilised by the rain and produces cereals for the food of mankind and grass for pasture. In the *Antigone* of Sophocles the chorus sings:

'O love invincible, thou art both he who descends upon our flocks and he who is ever on the watch from the blooming cheeks of our maidens. Thou movest upon the face of the waters and amid the lairs of wild beasts. And of the gods themselves, as of transitory mortals, not one can escape thee. He whom thou touchest straightway runs mad. Thou leadest the virtuous into evil courses, to their ruin.'

Accordingly, like Aphrodite, Eros is the personification of an elementary force of nature and a cosmic divinity.

Yet he was also represented by the Greeks, who do not seem to have troubled themselves about the strange contradiction involved, as a young boy, the son of Aphrodite. According to M. P. Nilsson he is a 'pretty little rascal' about fifteen, with a teasing and roguish disposition. As a rule he is winged and carries a quiver, a bow and arrows. He is always ready to attack anyone he meets, even his mother. Eros, or rather the *Erotes* ('loves'), may be found literally all over vase-paintings and reliefs from the fourth century onwards. In the end almost all their original significance is lost and they become mere fashionable decorations. In Alexandrian art Eros is no longer shown with the features even of a lad. He is simply a chubby infant, recognisable only by his bow and quiverful of arrows, shafts symbolic of the stings of

Tanagra Figurines of Eros. Heliog. Dujardin. Imp. Eudes, Paris. *New York Public Library.*

Aphrodite Riding the Waves in a Chariot Drawn by Two Erotes. Terracotta relief. *The Metropolitan Museum of Art, Rogers Fund, 1910.*

amorous desire. The Romans called this child Amor or Cupido.

Such 'Loves', with great outspread wings, were sometimes accompanied, in paintings of late date, by female children with butterflies' wings. These figures typified Psyche, the human soul, which was frequently represented as a small winged being, bird or butterfly. The tale of Eros and Psyche related in the *Metamorphoses* ('The Golden Ass') of Apuleius is well known. The subject is the 'invisible husband' of folklore, in which a fascinating prince only assumes his true form at night. As soon as Psyche, with very natural curiosity and in disobedience to the orders given her, turns her lamp upon Eros as he lies invisible beside her, he vanishes.

The arch and graceful yet formidable figure of the Alexandrian Eros appears in the poems attributed to Anacreon, or his imitators. The latter seem to have composed their light and witty verses in the Alexandrian age or even under the Roman Empire. The songs were current in the name of Anacreon of Teos, an Ionian poet of the sixth century B.C. He was mainly inspired by Aphrodite and Dionysus, in other words by the pleasures of love and wine. The Pléiade, a group of French poets associated with Ronsard, imitated this kind of poetry in Renaissance times.

Modern authors in general and even some ancient writers tend to confuse their personifications of Aphrodite and Eros. For both mother and son, after all, symbolised love.

But as a rule the Greeks distinguished the two deities very clearly. Aphrodite was regarded as the goddess of the physical act of sexual intercourse, while Eros figured as the god of erotic sentiment.

The philosophers who favoured homosexuality considered Eros to be in a special sense the god of the lover and his beloved. But in theory at any rate the affection between such persons remained pure friendship. Athenaeus in the *Deipnosophistae* writes:

'The Athenians were so far from thinking that Eros had

anything to do with carnal union that they erected a statue
to him in the Academy, a building dedicated to the virgin
goddess Athena, and offered sacrifices to both deities at the
same time.'

The same author also observes: 'The *Myrmidons* of
Aeschylus dealt with the love of Achilles for Patroclus, and
the *Niobe* of Sophocles is about homosexuality.'

In the Loeb text of Athenaeus the American editor
remarks that this information seems to contradict the famous
line in the *Frogs* of Aristophanes, where Euripides tells
Aeschylus: 'There's nothing about Aphrodite in your works,
that's certain!' True. But an ancient Greek would not
consider that Aphrodite was concerned in a tragedy about
homosexuality. He would refer it to Eros.

For that god presided primarily over the passionate
devotion of a grown man to a boy, Aphrodite over the sexual
relations between man and woman. Secondarily, however,
the conception of Eros could be extended to cover any
amorous feelings whatever, for both women and boys. In the
same way the conception of Aphrodite might cover either
normal or homosexual carnal intercourse.

Nearly all the legends about Greek heroes include pathetic
or tragic love-stories.

As already mentioned, the terrible fate that afflicted the
Atridae originated in the curse of Myrtilus. A charioteer in
the service of King Oenomaus, he was in love with the king's
daughter Hippodamia. She persuaded him to remove the
linch-pin of a wheel on the king's chariot before the race
against Pelops, who was her favoured suitor. Oenomaus was
killed by a fall from the chariot. Pelops carried off Hippodamia and slew Myrtilus, who died cursing the house of the
victor.

Other heroes were subjected to prolonged ordeals on
account of a woman's love. Bellerophon, for instance, was
beloved by Stheneboea, wife of Proetus, King of Tiryns, at
whose Court the hero had taken refuge. When Bellerophon

rejected her advances, she complained to Proetus that his
guest had offered her violence. The credulous Proetus sent
Bellerophon to the Court of Iobates, the king's father-in-law,
in Lycia, with a secret message requesting that the bearer be
put to death. Iobates directed Bellerophon to fight first
against the Chimera and then against the fierce Solymi,
hoping that he would be killed. But the hero triumphed over
all his adversaries by the aid of his winged horse Pegasus.
More fortunate than Hippolytus, he is even said to have in
the end revenged himself upon Stheneboea.

The misfortunes of the Labdacidae resembled those of the
Atridae in having begun with a love-affair. But this time the
love was homosexual. Laius took refuge at the Court of
Pelops, where he fell in love with the latter's son, a handsome
youth named Chrysippus. He carried off the boy, thus
providing Greece with its first instance of pederasty, which
had formerly been unknown. Pelops cursed the ravisher,
with the result, as everyone knows, that Oedipus, the son of
Laius, was fated to kill his father and marry his mother.
After the death of Oedipus the curse continued to afflict his
family. His sons Eteocles and Polyneices killed each other in
a fight for the throne of Thebes. The king, Creon, forbade
Oedipus's daughter Antigone to bury Polyneices. But she did
so and was condemned to be walled up in a cavern. Then
Creon's son Hemon, who had been in love with her, tried to
kill his father, failed, and committed suicide. His mother
Eurydice also killed herself, in despair at her son's death.

The seer Tiresias played an important part in these events.
In the *Oedipus Rex* and then in the *Antigone* of Sophocles he
gives advice to Oedipus and subsequently to Creon, which is
disregarded. An extraordinary adventure had happened to
him. Once on a journey he had seen two snakes mating. He
separated them with his staff but in so doing wounded them.
He was instantly turned into a woman. Seven years later he
saw the same two snakes copulating, again separated them
with his staff and at once returned to masculine form.

Zeus and Hera, who was both his wife and sister, were said to have been arguing one day as to whether male or female experienced the keenest physical pleasure in love. They called upon Tiresias, who had been both man and woman, to decide the question. He had no doubt about it. In his opinion female enjoyment of the act was exactly nine times as great as male.

Caenis, like Tiresias, had been first of one sex then of the other. To begin with, as a woman beloved by Poseidon, she had requested the god to turn her into a brave, invulnerable man. Poseidon did so and she took part in the battle against the Centaurs. They could not kill her, so they buried her alive. She then either returned to feminine form or became a bird with shining wings, a flamingo or phoenix.

Amphiaraus was a seer like Tiresias. He foresaw that if he joined the expedition of the seven chieftains against Thebes he would perish. So he refused to go. But Polyneices, anxious for his assistance, bribed his wife Eriphyle to persuade him to change his mind. The present offered was a magnificent necklace which had belonged to Harmonia. In return for this gift Eriphyle prevailed upon her husband to leave for Thebes, much against his will. He died there, as he had foreseen, a victim of his wife's vanity.

But in many legends the male partner is to blame. King Tereus had married an Athenian named Procne, the daughter of Pandion. She had given him a son called Itys. Later on Tereus fell in love with Philomela, the younger sister of Procne, and violated her. Then, to prevent her revealing his crime, he cut out her tongue. But she embroidered the tale of her wrongs on a piece of cloth, which she showed to Procne. The two sisters then took vengeance on Tereus by slaying his son Itys, whereupon Tereus pursued them with a drawn sword. But Zeus turned Philomela into a nightingale, Procne into a swallow and Tereus into a hoopoe.

A dramatic story of love and death is illustrated by a splendid vase-painting. The Amazon Penthesilea came to the help of Priam and his people before Troy. She challenged Achilles. But he ran her through with his sword. As she fell, their eyes met. 'Achilles recognised in her a woman worthy of him, his equal, a being of his own kind. He was stricken with a sudden overwhelming love for her. But it was too late. She was already dying in his arms. The hero, frantic with grief, found that he had killed the woman he loved and that she would now never be his. . . . He burst into bitter tears and loud lament.' (G. Méautis, *Mythes Inconnus de la Grèce Antique*, Albin Michel, 1944, pp. 70–71.)

Perseus, the son of Zeus and Danae, was luckier. While travelling in Ethiopia he saw Andromeda fettered to a rock as a sacrificial offering to a sea-beast. First pitying and then falling in love with her, he promised her father to rescue the girl on condition that he received her hand in marriage. The bargain was struck. Perseus killed the monster and wedded Andromeda.

The greatest of the heroes, Heracles, was by no means a paragon of virtue. Having married first Megara and then Deianira he allowed Omphale, Queen of Lydia, to purchase him as a slave and became her lover. Dressed in a woman's long robes he sat at her feet learning to spin, as if he had changed his sex like Tiresias and Caenis. Nevertheless, his sexual exploits were famous in Greece. It was believed that he had ravished the fifty virgin daughters of Thestios in a single night (Pausanias, IX, 27, 6–9). As Plutarch comments in his *Erotikos* (761 D): 'It would be a labour of Hercules to enumerate all his love-affairs, so many were they.' On the hero's return from Lydia he added to his household a concubine named Iole, the daughter of Eurytus. Thereupon Deianira's jealousy grew so intense that it eventually caused his death on Mount Oeta from the agonies inflicted by a poisoned shirt which, the Centaur Nessus had informed Deianira, would restore the love of her husband. Nor did Heracles stop at women. He was 'ambidextrous', as the Greeks used to say, i.e. bisexual. He had an affair with his young nephew and companion Iolaus. The latter's tomb at Thebes, accordingly, became the scene of ceremonial oaths of fidelity sworn between male lovers. Heracles also fell in love with 'sweet Hylas, he of the curling locks' (Theocritus, *Idyll*, XIII).

But these stories may possibly have been invented at a somewhat later time, when the development of homosexuality had suggested its practice by the heroes. In the *Iliad* there are no physical relations between Achilles and Patroclus. But in the *Myrmidons* of Aeschylus the friends are also lovers. For in that tragedy Achilles reproaches his dead companion for not having loved him enough to survive:

'Despite our kisses, cruel one, to save
those lustrous thighs thou didst not think, alas!'

Plato remarks scornfully in the *Symposium* (180 a) that 'Aeschylus is talking nonsense when he makes Achilles the lover of Patroclus. For the son of Peleus was not only handsomer than Patroclus, but the best looking of all the heroes. Moreover, as he had not yet grown a beard, he was the younger of the two friends, as Homer himself states.'

As for Theseus, the Athenian rival of Heracles, the legend makes it clear that before he became a wise, liberal and almost democratic king, he had been a regular Don Juan, 'drawing all hearts to follow him' and quite unscrupulous. His friendship with Pirithous does not seem to have lent itself to such malicious gossip as the relations between Achilles and Patroclus or between Heracles and Iolaus. But Theseus won the love of Ariadne in no time, only to desert her at their first port of call. The worthy Plutarch has no difficulty in understanding how ready she was to forget her duty and throw in her lot with so handsome and noble a hero.

'The love of Ariadne,' he writes, 'was the work of a god. We must not blame her for falling in love with Theseus. We should rather be surprised that all his contemporaries, men

(Top), Rape of Korone: Perithoos, Helen and Theseus. Detail of Amphora by Euthymides, c. 510 B.C. Glyptothek, Munich. *Griechische Vasen der Reisarchaischen Zeit,* Reinhard Lullies, Hirmer, Munich, Germany.

(Bottom), Theseus Overtakes Antiope. Vase-painting by Polygnotus II. Vatican Collection. Photograph by Alinari. *Der Lewismaler,* Henry Roy Williams, Heinrich Keller, Leipzig.

and women, did not follow her example.' (*Life of Romulus*,
30, 6–7.)

All the same, there is no excuse for the behaviour of
Theseus to Ariadne. Quite a number of his other love-affairs
too, those for instance with Phaedra and Antiope, 'began
with actions which we can hardly praise and ended in effects
which we can scarcely call happy,' as Plutarch himself
observes in his life of the hero (No. 29). Worst of all, Theseus
carried off Helen before Paris did so, when she was barely of
marriageable age and the hero himself had long passed that
of romantic folly. After this exploit he added sacrilege to
concupiscence by daring to accompany Pirithous to the
underworld in an unprecedented undertaking, the rape of
Persephone, wife of Hades himself.

It is clear that the heroes of mythology were not always
much more edifying characters than the gods and goddesses
of the *Iliad*.

When Theseus and Pirithous defied the terrors of Hell and
Cerberus to satisfy their lust, they were criminals who in the
end paid dearly for their presumption. But others who
contrived to pass those dreadful gates were impelled by a pure
and disinterested affection. There are three legends which
prove that the Greeks had meditated on the mysterious
bonds between love and death long before the chivalrous
society of the Middle Ages and such tales as that of Tristram
and Yseult, which in fact contains a good many reminiscences
of ancient writers. The Greek myths in question are those of
Orpheus and Eurydice, Admetus and Alcestis, Protesilaus
and Laodamia.

The enchanting singer Orpheus personifies the miraculous
powers of music and poetry. His voice, which he accompanied
on the harp, could charm the fiercest of men. Wild animals,
trees, plants and even the waves of the ocean were entranced
by his melodies. A fine vase-painting, for which the title
'The Triumph of Music' has been proposed, shows him
seated on a rock, playing a lyre. He is singing with parted
lips and head thrown back, his whole being absorbed in

Orpheus among the Thracians. Vase-painting c. 440 B.C. Berlin. *Die Bildnisse der Antiken Dichter*, Karl Schefold, Benno Schwabe, Redner und Denher, Basle.

inspiration. Four Thracians surround him, visibly enthralled by the divine melody.

When Eurydice, the wife of Orpheus, died, the inconsolable husband descended into the underworld to look for her. The gates of Hell, though inaccessible to the living, opened at the sound of his music. Cerberus and the other monsters, the infernal gods themselves, were spellbound by it. Hades and Persephone agreed to restore Eurydice to a husband capable of such proofs of his love. But they insisted on one condition. Orpheus could ascend to the upper air again, followed by his wife. But he must not turn to look back at her until he had left the underworld. Orpheus accepted the condition and had already almost reached the light of day when, in his anxiety and impatience, he glanced back. Eurydice instantly vanished, this time for good. An excellent relief in the Phidias Room at the Louvre illustrates the scene. But by a mistaken interpretation of it the names of Zetus, Antiope and Amphion have been engraved above the figures representing Hermes, Eurydice and Orpheus. The legendary singer later inspired the Orphic sect which maintained a secret cult of Dionysus. The first Christians sometimes depicted Orpheus in their catacombs as a genius who was believed to have foreseen the true destiny of humanity.

Orpheus failed in the end to achieve his purpose. But others succeeded in similar enterprises, though unaided by the magic power of music. For their love was greater than his. In the *Symposium* of Plato (179 c–d) Phaedrus observes that Orpheus did not die in order to follow Eurydice to the underworld. He preferred to enter it alive. But Alcestis, by agreeing to die in place of her husband, performed an action which 'seemed so glorious not only to mankind but also to the gods that they bestowed an extremely rare mark of their favour upon that noble woman. They admired her so fervently that they caused her to return from the underworld.

Admetus, King of Pheres in Thessaly, had a young, affectionate and devoted wife, Alcestis, who had already given him two children. He fell ill and could only be saved from death if someone offered to take his place among the dead. Alcestis alone consented to make the supreme sacrifice. She gave her life for her husband. In the tragedy by Euripides on this subject Admetus exclaims at her death-bed: 'Would that I had the melodious voice of Orpheus, that I might charm the daughter of Demeter'—i.e. Persephone— 'or her spouse, and thus rescue thee from the underworld, for then I would descend thither. . . .' Elsewhere he states: 'I will have an image made of thee by skilled craftsmen and lay it on my bed. I will take my place beside it and embrace it, calling upon thy name. I shall believe that I hold my own dear wife in my arms, though she will be absent. Alas, how cold a pleasure!'

Alcestis dies. But Heracles appears as a guest in the house of Admetus and is generously welcomed by the king, who hides his grief. Thereupon the mighty hero rescues Alcestis from the underworld. He brings her back veiled to Admetus, telling him that she will now only have to be purified of her consecration to the infernal gods and for that reason will not be able to speak to her husband for three days.

The ancient writers considered Euripides a woman-hater. Yet it was he who dramatised this sublime example of conjugal affection. He also dealt in the *Suppliant Women* with the suicide of Evadne, who refused to survive her husband Capaneus and flung herself from a high rock, like a Hindu widow of former times, on the funeral pyre. Euripides even composed a play on the story of Protesilaus. This work as a whole is unfortunately lost. But a few fragments survive.

Louis Sechan states in an article on the subject in *Lettres d'Humanité*, XII, 1953, p. 3, that 'the legend of Protesilaus, like that of Alcestis, originated in Thessaly, the country of magicians, mystery and miraculous love-potions'. Laodamia, wife of Protesilaus, was actually a niece of Alcestis. He had been the first casualty of the Trojan War. As he leapt ashore at the head of the troops he was struck down, mortally wounded. It so happened that he had set out on this expedition the very day after his marriage to Laodamia. The grief of the young couple was so heart-rending and their entreaties to the gods so pathetic that Hades permitted Protesilaus to return to the side of his beloved, though sadly enough only for a few hours.

In one version of the legend Laodamia kills herself in her husband's arms when the time comes for him to return for ever to the infernal regions. In the variant followed or invented by Euripides she has a waxen image made of her husband, as Admetus had promised, in the case of Alcestis, that he would have one made of her. Laodamia proceeded to lavish all her affection upon the image of Protesilaus. When her father had it thrown into a furnace, she instantly flung herself after it.

When Protesilaus obtained permission to leave the underworld for his pitifully brief visit to Laodamia, he proved, in the words of the Roman poet Propertius, that 'great love brims the banks of death'. Such was the lesson also taught by the legends of Orpheus and Alcestis.

Plutarch writes in his *Erotikos* (761 E–F):

'Love teaches even women to defy death. If it is legitimate to draw conclusions from fable, the legends of Alcestis, Protesilaus and Eurydice the wife of Orpheus prove that Love is the only god from whom Hades accepts orders. He feels pity for lovers and for them alone ceases to be inflexible and implacable. Furthermore, though it may be of advantage to be initiated into the mysteries of Eleusis, I believe that the votaries of those of love have the better portion in the underworld. Some divine dispensation has enabled legends to hit upon the truth when they tell of lovers returning from the kingdom of the dead to the light of day.'

The mysteries of love are thus stated to be more effective than those of Eleusis in ensuring immortality. The former secrets are revealed to all lovers who know in their hearts that their love is stronger than death. This resolute faith of mankind was expressed in legends of great beauty by the ancient Greeks. Nor was this belief rejected by their philosophers, or not, at any rate, by those who, like Plutarch, relied on Plato. They saw in it the presentiment of a higher reality.

3

HOMOSEXUALITY

'Thyrsis and Corydon mingled the flocks that they kept.
The first had ewes, the second she-goats heavy with milk.
Both herdsmen were twin flowers of their Arcadian youth.'

VERGIL, Bucolics, VII.

THE word pederasty is derived from the Greek *paiderasteia*, meaning literally the love of boys. In English pederasty has come to signify almost exclusively the practice of sexual inversion. But in Greek literature *paiderasteia* is used to refer both to pure, disinterested affection and to physical homosexual relations. In the present chapter we shall employ the word in its Greek sense. It will therefore at times imply, as in the case, for instance, of 'pedagogic pederasty', perfectly honourable affection between an older master or tutor and a younger disciple or pupil. It is impossible to do otherwise without deviating from the ancient texts by a change which might distort their meaning. The reader would be well advised to bear in mind that we shall occasionally give 'pederasty' this extended connotation. For otherwise he may not fully understand what we have to say on so delicate a subject.

In the first place it appears extremely likely that homosexuality of any kind was confined to the prosperous and aristocratic levels of ancient society. The masses of peasants and artisans were probably scarcely affected by habits of this kind, which seem to have been associated with a sort of snobbery. The available texts deal mainly with the leisured nobility of Athens. But they may give the impression that pederasty was practised by the entire nation. The subject, however, of the comedy by Aristophanes entitled *Lysistrata* suggests that homosexuality was hardly rampant among the people at large (see below, p. 105). It would be an error of perspective to think so, and the mistake may as well be pointed out here and now. We shall return to it at the end of the present work.

There was nothing particularly 'Greek' about homosexual feeling. The nation in antiquity was by no means alone in providing illustrations of inversion, which has been practised at almost all times and in almost all countries. In our own day the productions of Verlaine, Proust and Gide, to mention only French writers, as well as a number of others, are sufficient evidence of the fact. In the pre-Christian era the case of Sodom is well known. Nor were the Persians, the Etruscans, the Celts or the Romans ignorant of homosexuality. But its existence among these peoples was kept more or less secret on account of the discredit which attached to it. But in Greece, though pederasty was forbidden by law in most of the cities, it had become so fashionable that no one troubled to conceal it. On the contrary, such tendencies were respected and even approved. Plato himself recommended their cultivation as a necessary preliminary to the successive stages of a philosophic understanding of Being.

Many Greeks, moreover, did not feel in the least ashamed of admitting that homosexuality was held in more honour among them than anywhere else in the world. They even affirmed that other nations which practised it were their pupils in this field. Herodotus, for instance (I, 135), alleges that the Persians learned the habit from the Greeks. Xenophon in the *Cyropaedia* (II, 2, 28) makes Cyrus ask:

'Is it your intention to teach Greek customs to that young man lying next you, since he is so handsome?'

In the previous chapter we noted a number of allusions to pederasty in the mythological legends current in the classical or Hellenistic ages. But in Chapter 1, dealing with Homer, we could find no trace of homosexuality in the *Iliad* or *Odyssey*, even in references to Ganymede. It is of course possible that Homer deliberately suppressed mention of a habit he deplored. For his poetry is well bred. His realism is always selective and never slips into vulgarity. There are, moreover, many other matters which he discreetly refrains from specifying.

Nevertheless, it seems quite likely that pederasty was not introduced into Greece, or at any rate did not prevail there to any great extent, before the Dorian invasions. For in historical times, as we shall soon see, it flourished mainly and attracted most attention among the populations of Dorian descent. Homer describes the Achaean and Mycenean civilisations of the thirteenth and twelfth centuries B.C., the age of bronze. To all appearance it was the Dorian invaders of the eleventh century B.C. who introduced into Greece both the use of iron and homosexual practices. H.-I. Marrou, however, in his *Histoire de l'Éducation dans l'Antiquité*, pp. 56–7, is of the contrary opinion.

In any case the Greeks themselves considered that pederasty was of relatively recent origin among them. In the *Erotes* attributed to Lucian there is a dialogue in which the defender of homosexuality admits that it is not a very ancient custom.

'At former epochs,' he says, 'male love-affairs were unknown. In those days it was thought indispensable to couple with women in order to preserve the human race from extinction. . . . Only with the advent of divine philosophy did homosexuality develop. We should be careful not to condemn an invention merely because it came late. . . . Let us agree that the old customs arose from necessity, but that subsequent novelties due to the ingenuity of man ought to be more highly regarded.'

In Plutarch's *Erotikos*, on the other hand (751 F), the champion of heterosexual love exclaims:

'Homosexuality resembles a son born late, of parents past their maturity, or a bastard child of darkness seeking to supplant his elder brother, legitimate love. For it was only yesterday or at best the day before yesterday that the pederast came slinking into our gymnasia, to view the games in which youths then first began to strip for exercise. Quite quietly at first he started touching and embracing the boys. But gradually, in those arenas, he grew wings—' Eros being always represented winged—'and then there was no holding him. Nowadays he regularly insults conjugal love and drags it through the mud!'

This passage by Plutarch notes an important fact. There can be no doubt that the development of homosexuality was connected with the rise of gymnasia and arenas in which boys practised the five exercises of the *pentathlon*, which comprised wrestling, the foot-race, leaping, throwing the discus and hurling the javelin. Others were boxing and the *pancration*, a mixture of fist-fighting and wrestling. The competitors were always naked and watched by admiring spectators. In the same work (749 F) Plutarch tells us that Pisias, in love with a certain youth, Bacchon, whom a rich widow wanted to marry, 'imitated ill-conditioned lovers of the ordinary sort in trying to prevent his friend from marrying. The man's only object was to prolong the pleasure he took in watching the boy strip in the arena, while he still retained his virgin beauty.' Most gymnasia contained not only a statue of Hermes but also one of Eros. We have already quoted Athenaeus to the effect that there was an image of Eros at the Academy, which was the gymnasium in which Plato met his disciples.

The Greeks were at all times, as we noted in the case of Homer's Helen, most sensitive to physical beauty, whether masculine or feminine. This susceptibility was felt even in the most ascetic of friendships, when the lover desired nothing more from his beloved than the pleasures of the eye. It should be borne in mind that women were almost entirely excluded from Greek social life, which resembled a man's club. This was especially so at Athens, for at Sparta girls and women had more freedom of movement. In the following chapter,

dealing with marriage customs and the lives of women confined in the *gynecea*, we shall dwell more explicitly on the
extraordinary fact, so amazing at first sight, that many of the
ancient Greeks lavished all their sexually rooted affections
upon boys. For they considered members of the other sex
inferior beings, lacking all education and refinement, good
for nothing but to ensure a posterity.

It was in the arenas above all that 'special friendships'
were formed. Moreover, if Plato's dialogues are to be credited
in this connection, on certain festive occasions the establishments in question were the scenes of positive Courts of Love,
in which youths and mature men discussed 'Cupid's
country', as it came to be called in later times. In the *Lysis*
Socrates meets a certain Hippothales, whom he immediately
recognises as a lover. For Socrates, as he himself declares, is
an expert in such matters. The philosopher asks the other
whom he loves. Hippothales blushes and refuses to answer.
He is too modest and timid to say. But one of his friends
reveals the secret.

'It's all very well, Hippothales,' he says, 'to blush and
stammer over the name. But Socrates will need no more than
a few seconds of talk with you before you deafen him with
incessant repetitions of it.' Turning to the philosopher, he
adds: 'As for us, Socrates, we are perfectly sick of hearing
the name of Lysis. Our ears are quite stunned with it. The
moment Hippothales has taken a few drinks, he starts singing
it out at such a rate that when we wake up next morning we
think we can still hear it. . . . Worst of all, he sometimes takes
it into his head to recite his verse and prose compositions to
us. He thunders out his love-songs in such terrifying tones
that we can't get away from them. Yet now he blushes when
you ask him with whom he is in love!' (204 c–d).

The group formed by Socrates, Hippothales and their
companions then visits the arena where Lysis practises. It is
a feast-day.

'When we came in,' said Socrates, 'I saw that the boys

had just finished sacrificing and were playing at knuckle-bones in their festival costumes. Most of them were in the courtyard. But some were in a corner of the dressing-room. They were taking knuckle-bones from a basket and playing at odd and even with them. Others stood round in a circle watching. Among these last Lysis attracted general attention. He was standing in a group of boys and young men with a crown on his head which he had worn for the religious ceremony. His bearing not only justified his reputation for beauty but showed that he was also "fair and good", that is to say, of a noble nature.' (206 e, 207 a.)

Lysis, with charming timidity, hesitates to join the group with Socrates. For the youth had caught sight of Hippo-thales, his lover, with them. But at last he decides, supported by a companion, to approach. Conversation begins. It is entirely on the subject of *philia*, a name which in Greek was applied to all affectionate sentiments, whether in the family or elsewhere. The English word friendship is a very imperfect translation of it. The most important point at issue was, who best deserved the glorious name of *philos*, the lover or his beloved. The question was also raised whether flattery of a beloved person won him over or on the contrary aroused his contempt.

All the same, at Athens a whole body of laws existed for the purpose of restraining the spread of pederasty. This legislation probably dated back to the time of Solon. It aimed among other things at keeping male lovers out of the schools and exercising arenas so far as possible. (See Aeschines, *Against Timarchus*, 9–11.) But laws can do very little to suppress widely disseminated and inveterate habits.

In most of the Dorian States homosexuality appeared more conspicuously than it did at Athens. The reason is easy to understand if we accept the theory that pederasty origin-ates in the comradeship of soldiers. (See H.-I. Marrou, op. cit.) For it was in the Dorian cities that preparations for war were of the greatest importance. Boys from the age of seven

upwards were enrolled in children's 'trained bands' and lived
in continuous contact with their elders at meals and in the
dormitories. Plutarch (*Erotikos*, 761 D) states: 'It was chiefly
warlike peoples like the Boeotians, Lacedemonians and
Cretans, who were addicted to homosexuality.'

According to Ephorus a male lover in Crete would declare
his feelings to the relatives and friends of his beloved. If they
consented, he would carry the boy off three days later, just
as at Sparta the bridegroom would simulate abduction of the
bride. The Cretan lover conducted the lad to his house, gave
him a present and then took him to some rural retreat for
two months, on a sort of honeymoon. After this period the
couple returned to the city, where the boy was given by his
lover a military outfit, a drinking cup and a bull, which the
youth had to sacrifice. These customs were no doubt
survivals of former puberty rites.

It was considered shameful in Crete for a well-born boy
not to have a lover. But lads who had already been abducted
were subsequently regarded with great respect.

Xenophon (*On the Constitution of Sparta*, 11, 12) reports that
in Boeotia men and boys likewise paired off in actual
marriages.

At Sparta itself 'boys who had reached the age of twelve
and had a good reputation obtained faithful lovers . . . who
shared in the good or bad opinion held of the children. It
is said that on one occasion when a boy had let fall a vulgar
expression his lover, not himself, was punished by the
magistrates.' (Plutarch, *Life of Lycurgus*, 17–18.) We shall
return to this 'educational' side of pederasty, which is
extremely important.

The age of a beloved boy seems always to have been
between twelve and twenty. A Greek epigram declares:

'Desirable is the bloom of a boy of twelve. But that of
thirteen is much more delightful. Even sweeter is the flower
of love that blossoms at fourteen years. Its charm increases
still more at fifteen. Sixteen is the divine age. A boy of

seventeen I would not dare to woo. Zeus alone would have the right to do so.'

As a rule the first signs of down on the chin of the beloved deprived him of his lover. But there were exceptions to this convention. Plutarch writes in his *Erotikos* (770 B–C): 'It is generally believed that a single hair would be enough to cut the amorous connection in two like an egg and that lovers of boys resemble nomads who set up their tents in green and flowery meadows in the spring but desert it as if it were hostile territory once the season is over. Yet we may recall a famous phrase of Euripides, spoken amid kisses and caresses to the handsome Agathon, who had already grown a beard: "Beauty is still fair even in its autumn".'

This particular Agathon was a tragic poet, like Euripides himself. It is he who, in Plato's *Symposium*, plays host to the guests he has invited to celebrate the success of one of his plays. He was also mocked in the *Thesmophoriazusae* of Aristophanes, one of his guests on that occasion, for his effeminate tastes. He was said to have worn a long robe, a saffron-coloured tunic and a cape, as though he were a woman, also a bust-bodice, a hair-net and tight buskins such as smart women affected. He is alleged, too, always to have had a mirror and a razor on him. The latter implement was in those days a typical accessory of the feminine toilet, rather than the masculine. For men wore beards, while women of fashion shaved off their superfluous hair. Agathon's prolonged love-affair with Pausanias, another of the guests at the *Symposium*, was celebrated throughout ancient times.

As a rule the lover in these associations was a mature man less than forty years of age. But Aeschines was forty-five when he made his speech *Against Timarchus* (No. 49), observing (136–7):

'I myself no more disdain the pleasures of love today than I did formerly. I freely confess it. . . . To be fond of good-looking and well-behaved young people is a natural tendency of all sensitive and liberal minds.'

The poet Sophocles, again, had passed fifty when he attended a banquet in Asia Minor during the expedition to Samos in which he shared the military command with Pericles. According to P. Mazon (*Les Belles Lettres*, 1955, p. x) on that occasion he 'gaily discomfited a certain pedant by teasing a boy cupbearer and turning the joke against himself by swearing he was a better strategist in love than in war'. Pericles himself was not homosexually inclined. He cared for no one but Aspasia. Sophocles, during the same expedition, happened to praise in his presence the beauty of a certain youth. But Pericles sternly rebuked him, so Plutarch reports in his life of the statesman (8, 8): 'A General, Sophocles, should refrain not only from soiling his hands but from contaminating his eyes.'

If we are to believe Athenaeus (XIII, 605), the poet was sixty-five when he experienced the following misadventure. 'One day he left Athens with a handsome boy, intending to take his pleasure with the lad. The boy laid his own shabby cloak on the grass and they covered themselves with the poet's own fine warm woollen cloak. After the consummation of the affair the youth seized the cloak of Sophocles and made off with it, leaving his own in its place.'

This incident, it appears, elicited an exchange of pungent epigrams between Sophocles and Euripides. We need only add that the former's habits by no means prevented him from being considered throughout classical antiquity as a man of exemplary piety, 'beloved of the gods'. The domains of religion and sexual morality were then regarded as completely separate. It was certainly not in the name of religion that Pericles, himself a 'free-thinker', addressed the above-mentioned reproach to Sophocles. The reference was simply to the dignified conduct expected of a high State functionary. In any case the mighty gods of Olympus themselves, from Zeus and Apollo downwards, were represented in classical times as ardent pederasts.

Homosexual love, like heterosexual, affected the whole

mind of the lover if the sentiment was strong. He paid assiduous court to the object of his choice and sometimes ruined himself by making all sorts of gifts to the lad. Such behaviour was known as the 'chase' of love. Plato, in the *Symposium* (183 a), mentions 'everything that lovers do for the boys they cherish, the prayers and entreaties with which they support their suit, the oaths they swear, the nights they spend on the doorstep of the beloved one and the slavery they endure for his sake, which no real slave would put up with'. Plato also refers in the *Phaedo* (73 d) to the profound agitation which lovers feel at the mere sight 'of a lyre, a garment or any other object in constant use by their loved ones, any of which are enough to call up the image of their darling, even if he is absent'.

In Xenophon's *Symposium* Critobulus describes his love for the young Clinias in forcible terms:

'I would rather look at him than anything else in the world. I would cheerfully agree to be blind to all other objects. I resent night and sleep because they remove him from my sight. I am grateful to the sun and daylight because they allow me to behold him. . . . Though I am fond of luxury I would rather give all my possessions to Clinias than receive their equivalent from someone else. I would prefer slavery under Clinias to my freedom as a citizen, and work for his sake to rest for my own. . . . I would follow him even through fire. His image is so deeply graven in my heart that if I were a painter or sculptor I could produce an absolutely faithful portrait or bust of him in his absence.'

Anytus, who was later to prosecute Socrates, fell in love with the handsome Alcibiades. At a splendid banquet given by the former, Alcibiades suddenly appeared with a gay throng of companions—as he did at Agathon's house according to the text of Plato's *Symposium*—seized about half of the valuable wine-cups standing on the table and ran off with them. The guests, much annoyed, commented to Anytus: 'What insufferable insolence!' But Anytus simply

retorted: 'Say rather that he has been generous. For I would have let him take the lot and yet he has left me all these!' (Plutarch, *Erotikos*, 762 C.)

As a frequently quoted Greek proverb has it: 'Among friends everything is held in common.'

The lover followed his beloved about everywhere, sometimes spent the night in front of his house, serenaded him, composed verses and songs in his honour, carved his name on walls, doors and trees, hung up garlands of leaves or flowers, like religious offerings, in his porch, and sent him all kinds of presents, such as fruit, a bag of knuckle-bones, a cock, a hare or a dog, as well as painted vases on which the artist had been instructed to engrave the boy's name, followed by the adjective *kalos*, 'fair'. Many such vases have survived. On the Acropolis at Athens a small stone cut to the shape of a wedge was discovered. It bore an inscription of the fifth century B.C. which read: 'Lysitheos declares that he loves Mikion more than all the other boys in the city, for he is

Greek Youths. Vase-painting.
New York Public Library.

courageous.' (Coll. Inscr. Graec., Ed. 3, 1266.)

This statement by a pederast is a simple avowal of affection based upon a laudable motive. There is nothing coarse about it, as there was in so many which were cut at an earlier date on the rocks near the gymnasium in the island of Thera, now Santorin, in the Aegean Sea. (See *Sammlung Griech. Dial. Inskr.* 4787–4797.)

In the game of *kottabos* played at banquets after the pouring of libations the lover threw the dregs of his wine in the direction of a copper basin, calling aloud upon the name of his beloved. If the drops fell into the receptacle the omen was favourable and the player would expect that his love would be returned.

When two or more lovers courted the same youth they felt the same kind of mutual jealousy as would be experienced by the lovers of a girl. Plutarch in his life of Themistocles (3) reports the rumour that the hostility between that distinguished statesman and the equally illustrious Aristides originated in the love of both these politicians for the same lad, the handsome Stesilaos of Ceos. According to the *Phaedo* of Plato (232 c and 239 d) the jealousy of the successful lover would cause him to deprive his beloved of all society other than his own and render him 'destitute of friends'.

The prosecutor in the speech composed by Lysias for delivery against Simon begins as follows: 'You may well consider love for a young lad to be unreasonable in a man of my age. But I beg you not to conceive a bad opinion of me. For we are all slaves of passion, as you know. . . . Both Simon and myself fell in love with the youth Theodotus of Plataea. But while I hoped to advance my suit by treating him with consideration, Simon believed he could force the boy to submit to him by violent and cruel means. . . . Simon also claims that he gave Theodotus three hundred drachmae after drawing up a contract with him and that I alienated the lad's affections by my plots.'

The whole speech is full of Lysias's picturesque descriptions of the squabbling and rioting, both indoors and out, which broke out in consequence of the rivalry of the two lovers of Theodotus.

A beloved youth might also be jealous of his lover. When Alcibiades arrives at Agathon's dinner-party he notes with vexation that Socrates is sharing a couch with the host, whose reputation is decidedly that of a 'pretty boy', and tells the philosopher: 'Naturally, you moved heaven and earth to get a place next to the best-looking person here!' Socrates exclaims irritably: 'See to my defence, Agathon. For my love of that fellow is constantly getting me into trouble. Ever since I fell in love with him I'm not allowed even to glance at a single good-looking youth, much less talk to one. He gets jealous at once, envies me and permits himself unbelievable impudence to and abuse of me. I'm afraid that one of these days he'll positively go for me!' (Plato, *Symposium*, 213 d.)

Quarrels and brawls, and also tender reconciliations, were

common between such lovers and their loved ones. For 'even in disputes and disagreements a great deal of pleasure and delight may be found.' (Xenophon, *Hiero*, 1, 35.)

Many crimes of passion were committed in consequence of homosexual love-affairs. A few could be regarded as acts of heroism. For Greek tyrants were often murdered by young men whom they had seduced and who afterwards came to hate them. Archelaus, King of Macedonia, for example, was assassinated by Crateas, who had been his favourite. Alexander of Pherae was killed by Pytholaus. Plutarch reports (*Erotikos*, 768 F) that 'when Periander, tyrant of Ambracia, jestingly asked his "boy friend" if he were pregnant, the enraged lad drew a dagger and slew him.'

But the most celebrated of these stories is that of the Athenian tyrannicides Harmodius and Aristogiton, who enjoyed the reputation of champions of freedom, like that of Brutus in Rome. In 514 B.C. they killed Hipparchus, son of the tyrant Peisistratus and brother of Hippias, who had succeeded his father. The Sixth Book of Thucydides (54–59) tells the tale in detail.

'The daring feat executed by Aristogiton and Harmodius was the result of a chance development in a love-affair. . . . Harmodius was a lad of the most striking beauty. Aristogiton, a citizen of the middle class, had fallen in love and lived with him. Then Hipparchus, the son of Peistratus, made advances to Harmodius, who repulsed him and reported his behaviour to Aristogiton. The latter, incensed, and fearing that the all-powerful Hipparchus would try to achieve his purpose by violence, immediately resolved to take advantage of his own good standing by conspiring to overthrow the Government.'

Aristotle in the *Constitution of Athens* (18) relates the rest of the story.

'Hipparchus, disappointed in his amorous desire, made no secret of his furious resentment, which he showed in and out of season. Eventually he went so far as to prevent the sister of Harmodius from carrying a basket in the Panathenaic procession and abused Harmodius as an effeminate debauchee. Harmodius and Aristogiton, driven beyond endurance, recruited a number of accomplices and proceeded to active vengeance. When the Panathenaic procession began they lay in wait for Hippias on the Acropolis. For he was to receive the celebrants after Hipparchus had sent them on their way. But the two chief conspirators noticed one of their subordinates talking confidentially to Hippias. In the belief that they were being betrayed they decided to anticipate arrest. Accordingly, they left the Acropolis before the other conspirators were ready to move and attacked Hipparchus, who was mustering the procession near the Leocorium in the Potters' Quarter. They killed Hipparchus. Harmodius was cut down on the spot by the guards. Aristogiton escaped. But he was soon caught and subjected to prolonged torture, of which he died.'

After this event pederasty acquired fresh glory at Athens, being almost equated with love of liberty and hatred of tyranny, since Harmodius and Aristogiton had been lovers. They were extolled as heroes by poets, painters and sculptors for ever afterwards.

It is a fact that homosexuality made great strides both at Athens and elsewhere in Greece during the fifth century.

Solon, archon and reformer of the Athenian Constitution in 594 B.C., wrote verses which were quoted by the devotees of both homosexual and heterosexual love. The former called attention to the lines:

'Boys in the flower of their youth are loved;
the smoothness of their thighs and soft lips is adored.'

The pederasts argued that Solon only forbade slaves to practise homosexuality and gymnastics because by so doing he intended to encourage free men to engage in them. On the other hand, the advocates of heterosexual love quoted a couplet from another elegy by Solon, composed at a later date, in which he appeared to have renounced the love of boys for that of women, wine and song:

'The works of Cypris, Bacchus and the Muses
are the founts of joy which I prefer today.'

We shall be referring to Theognis later. Anacreon of Teos in Ionia was fond of handsome young men.

'Boy of the virgin's face, I love thee sore. But thou dost not listen to me. Thou knowest not that thou holdest in thy hands the reins of my soul.'

Anacreon sang of the charms of Cleobulus and Bathyllus.

The Athenian Aeschylus and the Boeotian Pindar were practically contemporaries. They were born in the sixth century B.C., but reached their maturity in the first half of the fifth. Both were confirmed pederasts. Aeschylus's tragedy, the *Myrmidons*, dealt with the friendship between Achilles and Patroclus in terms entirely different from Homer's.

As a young man Pindar fell in love with Thrasybulus and, at the very end of his life, with Theoxenus. In his Ode to the latter he wrote: 'I pine when I look upon the blooming youth of lads.'

The abundant surviving literature composed by the ancients in praise of pederasty always assumes it to be an affair of minds, not of bodies, a pure, 'Platonic' love, as we still call it today, from which carnality is excluded. It was declared that Eros in such cases would not tolerate the presence of his mother Aphrodite. For Eros, as we have already suggested, symbolised the passion of the soul and Aphrodite fleshly unions, whether homosexual or not.

Thus Xenophon writes in the *Constitution of Sparta* (11, 13, 14):

'When a virtuous Lacedaemonian took pains to make a true friend of a boy whose talents he admired and to take him for a companion, Lycurgus would praise the man and regard the relationship as the finest form of education. But

the Spartan lawgiver thoroughly disapproved of all desires
obviously concerned with the lad's person. As a result of
this view, lovers at Sparta were as little addicted to sensual
pleasures in the company of their loved ones as parents are
in relations with their children, or brothers with brothers.
Some people refuse, all the same, to believe such a thing. I
am not surprised. For in many of the cities carnal desire for a
boy is not unlawful.'

We may note that Xenophon himself expects his readers.
to be sceptical.

Plutarch makes no special reference to Sparta. He has all
Greece in mind in the following passage (*Erotikos* 752 A–B):

'Homosexuals, who claim that sensuality plays no part in
their affairs, do so because they are ashamed of themselves
and fear punishment. They have to have some excuse for
approaching good-looking boys, so they make a show of
friendship and virtue. They cover themselves with dust in the
arena, take cold baths'—warm baths were considered weak-
ening—'and frown heavily. They assume the outward airs of
a learned philosopher, so as to be on the safe side of the law,
and then at night, when everything is quiet,

"when the cat's away the mice will play!"

If there is nothing aphrodisiac about the company of boys
and Aphrodite is therefore absent, why talk of love? For
the gods have willed that Eros should assist her and share in
her power and glory so far as she allows him to do so.
Consequently, if there is such a being as an Eros without
Aphrodite, he must preside over feelings which resemble
intoxication without wine, produced by fig-juice or barley-
water. They can only give the victim a headache to no
purpose or fulfilment and soon turn to disgust and aversion.'

In spite of Plutarch, however, it is quite possible that many
such friendships between men and youths were perfectly
chaste. We saw just now that Alcibiades showed himself

intemperately jealous of Socrates. But later on, in a somewhat improper passage of Plato's *Symposium* (217 a–219 e),
Alcibiades himself relates an anecdote which may be called
'The Temptation of Socrates', where the common procedure
in such affairs is reversed. The young man in this case has
already been corrupted by a number of love-affairs. It is he
who makes advances—and very shocking ones—to the
mature man whose knowledge and wisdom he greatly
admires. 'I had supposed,' says Alcibiades, 'when I heard
him talk of the "flower" of my beauty, that I was in for a
windfall, a wonderful piece of luck. I thought that if I
allowed him to be familiar with me I should learn from him
everything he knew.'

Accordingly, he arranged to be alone with the philosopher.
But the latter was far from taking advantage of the situation
to speak of love. Alcibiades then invited him to take part in
some physical exercises, wrestling with him for instance.
This proposal recalls the important part played in pederasty
by gymnastics and the arena. Socrates agreed to the suggestion but still maintained his reserve. Thereupon the
younger man took even greater risks.

'I asked him to dinner, behaving exactly like a lover who
means to come to the point with his beloved. It was some time
before he would accept my invitation. But at last he consented to come. Nevertheless, on his first visit he rose to go
as soon as he had eaten. As I felt rather ashamed of myself I
let him depart there and then. But the next time he came I
exerted myself to entertain him with conversation far into
the night. Then, when he said he wished to leave, I objected
that it was very late and persuaded him to remain.'

After still more talk in the dark Alcibiades felt the moment
propitious for a final test.

'It was as though I had been shooting at him half the
night and I believed I had hit him. So I got up and, without
giving him time to object, I covered him with my cloak—for
it was winter-time—and flung myself down beside him under

the same old cloak that he has on this evening. I threw both my arms round his godlike person and spent the whole night in that attitude. . . . The most cunning of my efforts merely increased his triumph. For he disdained the "flower" of my beauty, scoffed at it and insulted it. . . . I call the entire company of heaven to witness that throughout that night I passed beside Socrates nothing more out of the way occurred than if I had slept with my father or an elder brother.'

One may wonder, however, how many replicas of Socrates there were in Athens or the rest of Greece.

The poet Aristophanes provides the clearest evidence of the character of his period. But it is necessary to take his exaggerations with a pinch of salt. For his exuberant comic spirit was more concerned to produce laughable caricatures than a precise picture of contemporary habits. He is given a strange speech, a sort of anthropological fantasy, to which we shall return later, in Plato's *Symposium*. The passage seems to be a defence of all kinds of love. Nevertheless, it appears evident enough from his comedies that Aristophanes was a determined opponent of homosexuality. In the very first of his plays, *The Guests*, now lost, we know that he contrasted a decently behaved young man with an invert, treating the latter to a flood of sarcasm. From the *Acharnians* to the *Frogs* he continually attacks both active and passive pederasts with the harshest abuse. They were called respectively *paedicones* and *pathici* at a later date by the Romans. Cleisthenes, Agathon—whom we have already met—and Cleonymus, together with several others, were thus pilloried by Aristophanes. He compares the perversion of his contemporaries, to their disadvantage, with the far purer morals, in his view, of the previous generation, that of the gallant 'veterans of Marathon'.

'In those days the gymnastics master compelled the boys, when they sat down, to stretch out their legs, so as to prevent any shocking exposure of themselves to the spectators. Again, when they rose, they had to smooth down the sand, so as not to leave any imprint of their masculinity to meet the eyes of lovers. Not one of the lads ever rubbed himself with oil below the navel, with the object of producing a soft kind of down, like that of a quince, upon his organs. Nor did any approach his lover with affected intonations and tempting glances.' (*Clouds*, 973–980.)

Manners may have been better, more refined, at that period. But were the morals of the age so superior as all that? The example of Harmodius and Aristogiton, dating back to the sixth century, and a good deal of other testimony, entitle one to doubt it.

In any case, when Aristophanes in the *Birds* (137–142) presents an Athenian of his own day dreaming of an ideal city, he makes him talk as follows:

'I should like to live in a town where the father of some pretty boy might come up to me and say angrily: "Well, this is a nice state of affairs, you damned swaggerer! You meet my son just as he comes out of the gym, all fresh from his bath and you don't kiss him, you don't say a word to him, you don't hug him and you don't feel his testicles! And yet you're supposed to be a friend of ours!"'

At Athens the morals of boys were protected not only by their fathers but also by legislation. The laws in question were summarised by Aeschines in his speech *Against Timarchus* (13–20).

'If a father, brother, uncle or tutor sells a boy to a man of licentious character, the child will not be prosecuted. But the two parties to the transaction will be charged, the one with delivering the boy and the other with having paid for receiving him. When the child grows up, he will not be obliged to provide his aged father with either food or shelter, since his parent had sold him into prostitution. The boy will be required only to bury his father in accordance with the usual formalities.

'The Law of Outrage stipulates that the assailant of a child, whether the victim be free or a slave, shall be charged

Schoolboy and Pederast. Red-figured vase by Polygnotus II. University at California at Berkeley. From Chiusi. *Der Lewismaler*, Henry Roy Williams, Heinrich Keller, Leipzig.

and the due penalty applied or else he shall pay a fine determined by the court.

'Any Athenian citizen who prostitutes himself shall be excluded from exercising any public function or even expressing his opinion in the Assembly or the Council. He will be charged with *hetairesis*'—lack of principle—'an offence punishable with the utmost rigour of the law'.

We learn from this passage that masculine prostitution, like feminine, existed at Athens. One might, indeed, already have suspected it from certain anecdotes related in the present work, especially that concerning Sophocles.

It was considered shameful, in cases of true and honourable affection, to allow oneself to be tempted by the wealth or even the political influence of a lover. (See Plato, *Symposium*, 184 a.) The favours of corrupt and venal persons, on the other hand, were bought for cash. But such youthful male prostitutes incurred general contempt. Plutarch (*Erotikos*, 768 E) states: 'Boys who voluntarily agree to act as accessories to debauchery of this kind are regarded as the most degraded of beings.'

Some were 'peripatetic', soliciting their patrons in the street or at cross-roads. They tried their hardest to attract attention by their dress and cosmetics, the object being to look as handsome and at the same time as effeminate as possible. They were so conspicuous that, in the words of a current proverb, it was 'easier to hide five elephants in one's armpit than a single invert'.

Such youths would follow a client to his house or submit to his caresses in the open air, at night, in deserted outskirts of the town, on Mount Lycabettus or even in the centre of the city itself, near the Pnyx.

Others, especially young and good-looking slaves, were kept by their masters in brothels and visited there by patrons. These houses paid an official tax annually confirmed by the Council. (See Aeschines, *Against Timarchus*, 119.)

But no further details of this unpleasant subject need be

noted here. Those who wish to pursue the matter may consult Appendix V of the work by the classical scholars Meier and Pogey de Castries on the physiology of homosexual practices in antiquity, *Histoire de l'Amour grec dans l'Antiquité*, pp. 292–302 (*Aristote et sa théorie scientifique de l'inversion sexuelle*).

We may more profitably return to the less disagreeable aspects of pederasty, which was also in a sense educational, as Xenophon asserts in the *Constitution of Sparta*, 11, 13, and as H.-I. Marrou, among others, has recognised. In his *Histoire de l'Éducation dans l'Antiquité* he devotes an excellent chapter, 'Pederasty as Education', to the topic.

Even in legendary times a hero who takes an interest in a youth is represented as taking pains to form his character and teach him manliness. Theocritus, in the idyll called *Hylas*, wrote:

'The son of Amphitryon, Heracles of the iron heart, who did not flinch from the savage lion, fell in love with a charming lad, Hylas of the curling locks. Heracles taught the boy, as a father would teach his favourite son, all that he himself had learned in order to be brave and worthy of a poet's song. He was ever at his side ... longing to fashion the youth in his own image, that he might end by becoming truly a man.'

It has been suggested in the foregoing pages that pederasty seems to have begun by being a 'communion of warriors'. On this view it is intelligible that the ancients saw the practice as encouraging valour and endurance, even in times of peace, as when, for example, it was desired to rid the State of a tyrant. For it is reported that the tyrant Polycrates of Samos had all the exercising arenas in the island burnt to the ground, believing that such 'hotbeds of comradeship were so many citadels erected against him and constituted a menace to his power'. (Athenaeus, XIII, 602 D.)

Affection between males had its origin in the gymnasium, where youths were trained in such techniques as hurling the javelin, which were really in the nature of preparation for active service. They were continued in military camps and finally practised on the actual field of battle.

'At Thebes, when a lad associated with a lover reached the age of enrolment, his protector presented him with a complete fighting outfit. Pammenes, who understood the character of masculine love, drew up his men in accordance with an entirely new principle. He set pairs of lovers side by side in the ranks. For he knew that love is the only unconquerable general. The tribe or the family may be deserted by their members. But once Eros has entered into the souls of a pair of male lovers no enemy ever succeeds in separating them. They display their ardour for danger and risk their lives even when there is no need for it. The Thessalian Thero, for instance, once laid his hand against a wall, drew his sword and cut off his thumb, challenging his rival in love to do the same. Another such lover, having fallen face downwards in battle, begged his enemy to wait a moment before stabbing him, lest the youth whom he loved should see him wounded in the back.' (Plutarch, *Erotikos*, 761 B-C.)

In a preceding passage of the same work (760 E-F) Plutarch describes the heroic death of Cleomachus of Pharsalia.

'The Chalcidians requested their ally Cleomachus, a man of splendid courage, to lead their troops to the attack. The youth whom he loved being present, Cleomachus enquired whether he intended to watch the assault. The lad answered in the affirmative, tenderly embraced him and set the helmet on his friend's head. Thereupon Cleomachus, his martial spirit raised to the highest pitch, called upon the bravest of the Thessalians to follow him, led them in a magnificent charge and threw the hostile cavalry into utter confusion. But he perished in the thick of the battle. The Chalcidians still show his tomb, surmounted by a tall column, in the main square of their city. They had formerly disapproved of homosexuality. But after the death of Cleomachus it found more favour among them than anywhere else in Greece. At a

later date the following verses were often sung by the
citizens:

> "Lads full of grace of every kind
> and virtues to your fathers' mind,
> scorn not the courtship of the brave
> who would your beauteous favours crave,
> For Love, our bodies' Lord, we see
> flowers with courage mutually
> in cities of Chalcidice.'"

Pederasty, in fact, was so widespread in Chalcis that the
common expression in the rest of Greece for acting as an
invert was to 'chalcidise'.

The famous 'sacred band' of Thebes was composed of
pairs of lovers. Such was even the reason, according to
Plutarch in his life of Pelopidas (18), why this unit was so
called, 'for Plato said that lovers were friends inspired by a
god'. The reference is to the *Phaedo*, 255 b. This body of troops
is stated to have remained invincible until the battle of
Chaeronea, where it was defeated by Philip of Macedon.
The latter, when he inspected the field after the engagement,
halted at the spot where the three hundred members of the
'band' had fallen. Every one of them had his wounds,
inflicted by pikes, in front. They had all retained their
weapons and lay close together. Philip was lost in admiration.
When he was told that they were all homosexuals, he wept
for them, exclaiming, 'Accursed be those who imagine that
such heroes could ever do or suffer a deed of shame!'

Plato makes Phaedo say in the *Symposium* (179 a–b):
'A handful of lovers and loved ones, fighting shoulder to
shoulder, could rout a whole army. For a lover to be seen by
his beloved forsaking the ranks or throwing away his weapons
would unquestionably be less bearable than to do so in the
presence of a crowd. He would a thousand times rather die
than be so humiliated. As for abandoning his loved one on

the field or refusing to rescue him when in peril, the worst of cowards would be inspired by the god of love on such occasions to prove himself the equal of any man naturally brave. For the gallantry which, as Homer says, a deity "breathes into the hearts of heroes" is truly a gift of Love to lovers, one which they owe to him alone.'

It is beyond dispute, therefore, shocking as the fact may appear, that 'homosexuality contributed to the formation of the moral ideal which underlies the whole practice of Greek education. The desire in the older lover to assert himself in the presence of the younger, to dazzle him, and the reciprocal desire of the latter to appear worthy of his senior's affection, necessarily reinforced in both persons that love of glory which has always appealed to the competitive spirit of all mankind. Love-affairs accordingly provided the finest opportunities for noble rivalry. From another point of view the ideal of comradeship in battle reflects the entire system of ethics implied in chivalry, which is founded on the sentiment of honour.' (H.-I. Marrou, *Histoire de l'Éducation dans l'Antiquité*, pp. 58–9.)

But the apprenticeship to courage and the love of honour and glory, important as they were to the Greeks, comprised only a part of Greek education. For lovers claimed that they participated actively in all the moral and intellectual development of their loved ones.

In the age of Pericles young Athenians attended schools in which they learned to read, write and calculate, as well as musical academies and gymnasia, where physical exercises were taught. Such was the elementary or, as we should say, 'primary' instruction provided. More advanced tuition and moral training in the full sense of the phrase had to be sought elsewhere.

In the second half of the fourth century the 'sophists' were the first to supply Greece with secondary education. They were sages who travelled about the country followed by the disciples whom they had attracted. They taught both the higher branches of knowledge and character-building. But their lessons were expensive and occasionally disappointing.

Family life could contribute little in this field. The 'pedagogue' who took charge of the children of rich families was a slave. He could teach his young master scarcely more than a few maxims acquired by experience or derived from folklore. The mother would be herself distinctly ignorant and in any case ceased to supervise her sons after the age of seven. The father could indeed, in most cases, attend to his sons' intellectual and moral discipline, if he felt genuinely impelled to do so and above all if he had the time. But he was always engrossed in public life and his own profession.

At the beginning of the *Laches* of Plato two worthy fathers of families are introduced. Lysimachus is the son of the great Aristides and his friend Melesias is the son of Thucydides, not the historian, but the political rival of Pericles. Both fathers want to find tutors for their sons, so as to give the boys a better chance than they had themselves. For, as Lysimachus remarks with touching humility, 'Neither of us is distinguished, since our illustrious fathers didn't take much trouble over our education. We're a bit ashamed of that in front of our sons. We blame our fathers for it. They let us run wild when we were young, as they were so busy with other people's affairs themselves.'

This serious gap in the Athenian curriculum was normally —if one can use such an adverb in referring to abnormal personages—filled by pederasts. For pederasty functioned as a branch of pedagogy, as both Xenophon and Plato testify, the older man being naturally at pains to develop the character of his pupil, his 'beloved', and pass on everything he knew to the boy, just as Heracles was said to have behaved in regard to Hylas, thus raising both his intellectual and moral standards.

The tradition was certainly an aristocratic one, since it allowed pederasts to transmit from generation to generation 'an exclusively male ideal, involving contempt for women', as H.-I. Marrou puts it. The practice is already clearly referred to in the didactic and elegiac verses of the sixth-century poet Theognis of Megara. They are addressed to a youth named Kyrnus, with the object of teaching him everything he ought to know and giving him a 'virtuous' character, in other words making him one of a select few. The devotion of Theognis to his disciple can be discerned in many passages, e.g.

''Tis for thy good, Kyrnus, that I shall lay down these precepts, just as I received them myself in my childhood from men of merit' (v, 27, 28).

He speaks, no doubt, 'as a father to his son' (v, 1049). But he also says:

'Be not content to cherish me in words alone nor divert unto others thy heart and thoughts if truly thou lovest me and thy soul keeps faith with mine. Thou must either love me without pretence or declare open war against me' (v, 87–90).

The poet's uneasiness was succeeded by a typical lover's grievance. For it seems that Kyrnus was slow to return his master's affection.

'In thee I find no smallest trace of care for me. Thou treatest me as a little child, with fine words only' (v, 253–4).

Just as Theognis adopts towards Kyrnus the attitude of 'a father to his son', so Socrates, according to Plato (*Apol.* 31 b), told his judges that he wished to act as 'a father and elder brother' to the Athenians. The phrase indicates the personal and intimate way in which such instruction was imparted. It was based entirely on friendly or loving relations, ties of profound affection, between master and disciple.

The *Memorabilia* of Xenophon are unquestionably more realistic than the dialogues of Plato in their details of the daily life of Socrates. It is clear that he was selflessly devoted to his friends. He willingly acted, in his own words, as 'agent' and even 'mediator' in their affairs. He organised among them a sort of mutual aid society. Xenophon gives a number of instances of the services thus provided, adding:

'Whenever his friends were in any difficulty, he did all he possibly could to show them how to help one another.' (*Mem.* 11, 7, i.)

In short, he interpreted literally the Pythagorean principle already cited, 'All is common among friends.' This idea played a leading part in Greek moral philosophy.

It was by no means confined, of course, to material considerations. Thoughts and feelings were also subject to it. For this reason Socrates claimed to have an expert knowledge of love. But he did not, like the sophists, represent himself as a master in it. For he used to say that there was only one thing he knew, and that was that he knew nothing. On the contrary, he professed to act only out of passionate friendship, entirely dedicated to the happiness of those he loved.

All the schools of ancient philosophy adhered to this noble principle. They were essentially societies of friends. Epicurus even made friendship a fundamental institution of his Garden.

This outlook no doubt resulted from a profound intuition. Teachers succeed only in so far as they love. Socrates affirmed that he loved, though in a purely spiritual sense, those whose minds he wished to develop. When he went in search of disciples, he said he was 'hunting down good-looking young fellows'. It was a widespread notion in ancient Greece that a tutor needed the stimulus of beauty in his fertilising operations. Plato regarded education as 'a spiritual bringing to birth of beauty' (*Symposium*, 206 b).

We shall return to these conceptions at greater length in Chapter 6. But it is important to stress at this point the disturbing factor introduced by the idea of beauty into Greek educational theory. For it was considered that a mysterious affinity existed between physical and moral excellence. The Stoics asserted:

'The wise should love the young. For the latter's beauty proves that they are well equipped for virtue.'

It may well be objected, however, that since not all young

Athenians were handsome, the education of the less attractive must have suffered.

The Greek philosophers all defined homosexuality with pedagogy in view. Plutarch (*Erotikos*, 750 D) declares:

'Love for a young and talented mind leads to virtue by the road of friendship.'

In the same author's life of Romulus Polemon says (30, 6):

'Love is provided by the gods to ensure the profit and well-being of the young.'

The Greeks mistrusted knowledge derived entirely from books. They suspected written notes of any kind even more. In their opinion the best teaching was always oral, a communication between minds by word of mouth. In this respect too Socrates supplied the outstanding example. He wrote nothing. He only talked, gaining his effects to some extent, no doubt, by his famous irony, but still more by the inspiration of his extraordinary personality and the utter devotion it elicited from his youthful disciples, including even Alcibiades, whose faults, however, he did not hesitate to censure. Any lover worth the name, therefore, was for the Greeks one who initiated others into the life of the mind and acted as their guide and model. At Sparta, moreover, he was held morally responsible for the behaviour of his loved one.

Socrates furnishes the supreme, almost inimitable, instance of a pedagogue actuated by love of the purest kind. After his time Plato became the lover—though apparently not in the 'Platonic' sense—of Alexis and Dion. Those who succeeded his nephew Speusippus as heads of the Academy were often selected, so to speak, in accordance with the principle of 'pederastic adoption'. Diogenes Laertius states that Xenocrates was the lover of Polemon, who in his turn fell in love with Crates. The Stoics followed the example of their founder Zeno in being for the most part ardently addicted to homosexuality.

We may conclude, with H.-I. Marrou, that:

'The relation between master and disciple always had

some resemblance in ancient times to a love-affair. In principle the instruction imparted was not so much technical as represented by the sum of all the pains taken by a tenderly solicitous elder to promote the development of a pupil fervently desirous of responding to such treatment by showing himself worthy of it.' (*Histoire de l'Éducation dans l'Antiquité*, p. 62.)

Theognis and many other Greek poets of more refined imagination flourished in the sixth century B.C. It was at the beginning of this period that a great poet reached maturity on the island of Lesbos. She was a woman named Sappho or Sapho, more correctly Psappho, of exceptional gifts, designated by Strabo (XIII, 617) as a 'marvel'. She alone wrote poems which all antiquity regarded as equal in merit to those of Homer. An epigram in the Greek Anthology, attributed to Plato (IX, 506), calls her the 'Tenth Muse'.

But it may at once be asked why Sappho should be mentioned in a chapter dealing with homosexuality. For the charges of 'sapphism' and 'lesbianism' levelled against her even in ancient times are regarded by many Greek scholars and historians as pure calumny. Her attachment to several of her pupils may well have been as 'platonic' as that of Socrates for his. Nevertheless, the present chapter is concerned as much with spiritual as with carnal affection. Consequently, Sappho appears entitled to a place in it. For there is no doubt that she was at least very powerfully attracted by many girls. But her inclusion here does not of course mean that she is to be considered one of the 'damned' women referred to by Baudelaire in his *Lesbos*, when he writes:

'Mother of Roman frolic, Greek delight,
Lesbos, where kisses like cascades descend,
Lesbos, where Phryne calls a Phryne to embrace,
Lesbos, the land of warm and languid nights,
—let stern old Plato bend his brows in vain—
where Sappho, poet-lover, acts the male.'

Personally, I have always thought the last line but one unaccountable. I cannot see for what reason Plato would have condemned either Lesbos or Gomorrha, when he showed such indulgence, and even addiction, to the practices of Sodom.

Sappho was born in the island of Lesbos, possibly at Eresos, but more probably at Mytilene. The population was Aeolian and its customs were undoubtedly very different from those at Athens. We may suppose, in particular, that Lesbian women still enjoyed the freedom which had been current in the Homeric age and that those who belonged to the aristocratic and wealthy class, if not others, had such opportunities for education as were open to boys, though the girls may have attended separate schools of their own. Sappho in fact ran a kind of 'Boarding School for Young Ladies', something like that kept by Mme de Maintenon at Saint-Cyr, though of course the principles observed and the objects in view at these two establishments could not have had very much in common.

In Plato's *Phaedo* (235 e) Socrates calls the poetess 'Sappho the beautiful' without the slightest suggestion of censure, thus contradicting Baudelaire's account of her. The epithet, it seems, referred solely to her admirable verses and highly attractive personality, comparable with that of Socrates himself. Yet he was snub-nosed, with protruding eyes, and rather stout. According to contemporary evidence Sappho was short and had a swarthy complexion. This somewhat repellent physique, however, was combined with great emotional ardour and an incomparable genius for poetry and music. Théodore Reinach, in his edition of the poems of Alcaeus and Sappho, published by the Universités de France, p.169, describes her as 'a dark, lively little woman, good-humoured and outspoken, keenly responsive to every natural instinct and emotional impulse, charmingly malicious, passionate in love and in addition an inspired poet and an accomplished musician of innovating tendencies.'

Sappho's school for aristocratic young women was in origin a religious foundation, like the other 'cultural' institutions of antiquity, for instance Plato's Academy. It was a kind of 'sorority' dedicated to the Muses, the Graces and Aphrodite, just as the Academy was later officially patronised by the Muses, Athena and Eros. Sappho herself named her establishment the 'House of the Servants of the Muses'. As is well known, *musike*, the art of the Muses, comprised not only actual music and dancing, but also all branches of intellectual study, both scientific and literary. Accordingly, the protection of those deities, presiding over the whole sphere of education, and added to the cult of the Graces (charm) and Aphrodite (love), implied quite an extensive curriculum.

It would be a mistake, however, to suppose that Sappho's pupils learnt music, dancing and poetry with a view to taking up those arts professionally. It would be a still greater error to imagine that they intended to become priestesses participating in the ritual worship of Aphrodite, the Graces and the Muses. The few poems and fragments, mostly, alas, mutilated, which survive of this writer's work, allow only the obscurest intimations of the character of her school. But André Bonnard seems to me to have given the best account of it, worth quoting at length, especially as it was published in a periodical and is therefore less accessible than a book. He wrote:

'The House of the Muses was no more an academy of music or art than the sorority of Aphrodite was a theological college. The goddesses honoured in Sappho's school were regarded as the original incarnations of an ideal of feminine beauty which she hoped the young women who lived with her would achieve. She wished to help them to do so when they went out into the world. To this end she organised their lives in common, their study of the arts, their devotion to Aphrodite and their cult of the Graces. She meant her pupils to marry. For she was married herself and the mother

of a little girl whom she compares with a bunch of chrysan-
themums and an armful of golden buds. The joy and
beauty of marriage, conceived as the supreme fulfilment of a
woman's nature, was the sole purpose of Sappho's training
of the young women entrusted to her charge. . . . Sometimes
the "Servants of the House of the Muses" would sing
choruses in honour of their goddesses at festivals in the city.
They were also invited by the Mytileneans to chant the
wedding song at marriage ceremonies in the capital and its
suburbs. . . . As soon as a new pupil arrived or another left
to get married, the occasion was duly celebrated. The
garden never had enough flowers for the garlands and
wreaths required. The headmistress would compose a song of
welcome to the new arrival or one of farewell to the departing
member of the school. Often such poems were love-lyrics. . . .
The poetic education imparted by Sappho in the fervent
stanzas descriptive of the omnipotence of Aphrodite, which
were sung in unison by the girls, was named Erotics by the
ancients, a philosophy of love. Her poetry is indicative of the
passionate friendships to which such teaching gave rise
between Sappho and her young disciples, under the burning
skies of the realm of Cypris. For the fiery longings of her
lonely spirit, stimulated by the beauty she had created and
augmented in those about her, were released in the verses
she composed. It is hardly possible to believe that if such
desires had been physically assuaged they would have been
so brilliantly reiterated in literary creation.' (*La Poésie de
Sapho*. *Lettres d'humanité*, V, 1946, pp. 32 and 34–5.)

In considering Sappho we have already been reminded of
Socrates. The ancients themselves in fact compared the
tutorial methods, both based on love, of the Lesbian and the
Athenian. A Platonic philosopher of the second century A.D.,
Maximus of Tyre, wrote (*Discourses*, 24, 7–9):

'The conception of love evolved by the poetess of Lesbos
is simply the "art of love" of Socrates. Both seem to me to
have practised friendship in the same way, she in dealing

with women and he in his relations with men. Alcibiades,
Charmides and Phaedo were for him what Gurinno, Athis
and Anactoria were for her. Similarly, just as Socrates
competed with rival teachers like Prodicus, Gorgias,
Thrasymachus and Protagoras, so also did Sappho strive
with Gorgo and Andromeda, whom she sometimes reviles
and sometimes cross-examines with relentless irony, exactly
in the manner of Socrates.'

We have already noted that the appreciation of beauty,
regarded as an essential quality by the Greeks, could both
stimulate and disturb the relations between master and pupil.
If this idea is borne in mind, the analogy between Sappho
and Socrates becomes still more striking. For both were
characterised by the same sensitivity to good looks in persons
of their own sex and both considered beauty the best
encouragement of adequate education.

Gurinno, Athis and Anactoria, the girls named by Maximus of Tyre as pupils of Sappho, and also Gongyla,
Arignota and some others, flit with the light grace of shadows
through her verses, as in the following fragments:

'The charm of Anactoria's bearing, her radiant features,
would give me more pleasure to see than all the chariots of
the Lydians and their armoured infantry charging to the
attack . . . (Fr. 27, v, 17-20).

'Mnasidica is even lovelier than the exquisite Gurinno.
Never did I yet meet, my sweet one, a more disdainful
beauty than thou. . . .'

These lines are all that are left of Fragment 72. Usually
we have no more than a broken phrase or two of Sappho's
poetry, sometimes only a few words.

Ardent desire, regret or jealousy are often evident, as in
Fragment 36:

'Return, I implore thee, Gongyla, clad in thy milk-white
tunic. Ah, what intense desire attends thy beauteous form!
No woman could but tremble at its seduction. And I
rejoice, for it is she herself, the Cyprian goddess, who hath

made thee thus to blame, she whom I invoke in prayer. . . .'

One of the most famous of her complete poems, often since translated into many languages, inspired both Boileau and Racine in some of the best lines of his *Phèdre*. An English version by Sir C. A. Elton may be quoted here.

'That man is like a god to me
who, sitting face to face with thee,
shall hear thee sweetly speak and see
      thy laughter's gentle blandishing.
'Tis this astounds my trembling heart.
I see thee lovely as thou art.
My fluttering words in murmurs start.
      My broken tongue is faltering.
My flushing skin the fire betrays
that through my blood electric strays.
My eyes seem darkening as I gaze,
      my ringing ears re-echoing.
Cold from my forehead glides the dew.
A shuddering tremor thrills me through,
my cheeks a green and yellow hue,
      all gasping, dying, languishing.'

The physical effects of erotic passion are expressed in these stanzas in so striking and yet at the same time so simple a manner that it became as celebrated as the finest passages in the *Iliad* and the most familiar of the choruses of Sophocles and Euripides. Many Greeks knew the ode by heart. Plutarch, for example (*Erotikos*, 763 A), playfully tells one of his young friends, Daphnis, recently betrothed to a certain Lysandra:

'My dear Daphnis, if Lysandra has not yet completely banished your former favourites from your memory, do please remind us of the verses in which the glorious Sappho declares that on beholding the girl she loves her voice fails, her body burns, she grows pale and is plunged into giddiness and bewilderment.'

Thereupon Daphnis immediately recites the poem.

Whether the attachment of Sappho to her pupils was really as chaste as has been alleged is a question that may fairly be asked after perusal of Fragment 1, an ode to Aphrodite, which may be the only one of her pieces to survive entire, and Fragments 74 and 172, which read respectively as follows:

> 'The moon has set, and the Pleiads.
> 'Tis midnight. Time passes.
> And in my bed I lie alone.'

and

> 'May this night last for me as long as two.'

The probably erotic character of this prayer has been discussed by F. Martinazzoli and J. Perret. H.-I. Marrou remarks that 'these tearful outcries of a jealous woman suggest passions very different from those of the spirit', and adds: 'The frankness and, if one may say so, the immodesty of some feminine lyrists—in French the comtesse de Die and Louise Labbé come to mind—confirm to the full the sensual nature of the love-affairs in question.' (*Historie de l'Éducation dans l'Antiquité*, p. 66.)

Ovid may indeed have been right to enquire: 'What did Lesbian Sappho teach girls but love?' (*Tristia*, II, 365.) J. Carcopino (*De Pythagore aux Apôtres*, Flammarion, 1956, p. 27) comments: 'Greek literature owes to Sappho the most memorable cries of love ever uttered by a human voice. But even in the lines which have been handed down to us by Longinus in his essay "On the Sublime" as examples of that style her genius is ablaze with the fires of her personal passion. Alcaeus called her "chaste Sappho, gently smiling". She once reminded a timid male lover that he must respect convention. But there can be no doubt that even in ancient times she was believed to have abandoned it and that her reputation, even then, offended the virtuous.' Well, the ancients were more capable of assessing it than we are. For they were able to read her entire works, while we only possess odds and ends of it.

Legends soon arose about so exceptional a figure. According to Strabo (X, 452) she was said to have committed suicide for love of a man named Phaon.

'On the island of Leucadia stands the temple of Apollo Leucatas, with a rock from which a leap into the seas is supposed to cure lovers. Menander asserts, "It was there that Sappho, mad with love for the over-haughty Phaon, was the first to throw herself from the summit of the crag, which is visible afar off".'

The leap from the Leucadian rock into the Ionian Sea afterwards came to symbolise immortality to the Neo-Pythagoreans, a sect secretly active in Imperial Rome, where their subterranean basilica was discovered in 1917, near the Porta Maggiore. The myth illustrated in their doctrine the passage, through total renewal, to eternal life in the Beyond. The high renown of the poetess linked her memory to such beliefs. For she seemed to have been an 'incurable' devotee of love. But if she did in fact drown herself in despair, it is rather more likely to have been, though she was married and a mother, for love of a girl than for the sake of a handsome young man.

She had rivals in Lesbos, who also maintained schools for girls, in particular Gorgo and Andromeda. Accordingly, Sappho's 'sorority' was not the only one. But if her verses had not been so beautiful as to have survived generation after generation, we should probably have remained in entire ignorance of the very special form taken by feminine education in Aeolian settlements.

During the Periclean age there was no question of any feminine education at all, either at Athens or elsewhere in Greece. But there is some reason to suppose that female homosexuality was not altogether unknown, at Sparta at any rate, if Plutarch is to be believed. In the life of Lycurgus

(18, 9) he writes: 'At Sparta love was held in such honour that even the most respectable women themselves became infatuated with girls.'

The speech by Aristophanes in Plato's *Symposium* (191 e) unfolds an anthropological fantasy designed to justify any kind of love.

'Women cut from the second, feminine sex', he says, 'don't pay the slightest attention to us men. On the contrary, it's women they are inclined to. That's the species to which the darlings of some ladies we know belong!'

In fact, it may have been quite natural—if we may use such a term in this connection!—for the division of society into two parts, male 'clubs' and female assemblies such as the *Thesmophoria* at Athens in honour of Demeter, from which men were excluded, to have favoured passionate associations between women. They would correspond with those between the other sex, as Gomorrha contrasts with Sodom. The fifth of Lucian's *Dialogues of Courtesans*, in which one of two women mentioned, Megilla, is a native of Lesbos, suggests that affairs of this kind were by no means rare.

Youths in the Palaestra Preparing Themselves for Athletic Exercises. Red-figured vase-painting c. 440 B.C. Berlin Antiquarium. *Bettmann Archive.*

4

MARRIAGE AND FAMILY LIFE

'In the young the constraining power of love exceeds that of geometry.'

PLATO

IN Chapter 1 we found no trace of misogyny in Homer. But Hesiod, who probably lived towards the end of the eighth century B.C., perhaps less than a hundred years after Homer, takes up a very different attitude in this connection. The *Iliad* and the *Odyssey* describe the Bronze Age civilisation, prior to the Dorian invasions. Hesiod, dealing with his own time, considers it to be the Iron Age, that of a fifth period which he believes to have succeeded the eras of gold, silver and bronze, followed by the heroic age.

'Would to heaven I had not been obliged, in my turn, to live among men of the fifth race, that I had died sooner or been born later. For now is the race of iron.' (*Works and Days*, 174–6.)

It should be noted that Hesiod was a peasant, living in the small village of Ascra in Boeotia, where the soil was unrewarding and he had to work very hard. Farming communities are not usually those in which women are regarded with the greatest courtesy and consideration. Such qualities are more in evidence at aristocratic courts like those frequented by the Homeric heroes when they were not away fighting. But in spite of this difference of social environment I am of opinion that Hesiod's testimony is valuable, even essential, for the understanding of the cultural evolution that took place in the Greek 'Middle Ages', between the Achaean and the archaic, subsequently classical, periods.

One of Hesiod's favourite legends is that of Pandora.

It is found in both his surviving poems, the *Theogony* and the *Works and Days*. Pandora was a maiden fashioned by the gods and endowed with every sort of attraction, by the command of Zeus, to punish men for their transgressions.

'When Zeus had created, instead of a blessing, this curse outwardly so fair, he led her to the dwellings of gods and mortals ... a deep pitfall, whence none shall escape, for mankind. Since from her there issued that execrable breed of women, a fearful scourge upon the earth. They endure not hateful poverty. Wealth alone pleases them. ... He who evades, by refusing marriage, the miseries that women bring upon us will have no support'—i.e. children—'in the wretchedness of his old age. No doubt he will not starve, so long as he lives. But after his death his property will go to relatives. On the other hand he whose fate it is to marry may perhaps find a good and sensible wife. But even then he will see evil outweigh good all his life, while, if he lights upon some foolish creature, he will bear within his breast a load of grief that will never leave his soul. His misfortune will be irremediable.' (*Theogony*, 585–612).

Hesiod implies, in short, that the only reason for marrying is to have children, or rather, as we shall see, an only son, to support his father in old age and inherit his goods. A similar intense hatred of women appears in certain passages of the tragedies of Euripides, which almost amount to saying that if we could only find some way of having legitimate sons without marrying we should be perfectly happy.

Yet in the *Works and Days* the poet's detestation of the other sex seems a little less marked than in the *Theogony*. The myth of Pandora is not so bluntly related in the former epic (42–105). He also writes:

'Lead a wife to thy hearthstone at the right age, neither much below nor much above thirty years. Such is the proper time to marry. A woman should marry in the fifth year after puberty. Marry a virgin, that thou mayst train her in discretion. Prefer one who dwells close by. But consider all her circumstances well beforehand, lest after marriage thou become a laughing-stock to thy neighbours. There is no better stroke of luck for a man than a good wife and no worse fate than a bad one, ever on the watch for scraps from the table, who roasts her man without fire, strong though he may be, and brings him to a premature old age.' (695–705.)

Hesiod's advice, accordingly, is to marry at about thirty a girl of sixteen. These ages for marriage were also considered normal in classical times.

In the *Works and Days* (373–5) he remarks: 'Don't let a woman, either, make you lose your head over her bedizened rump. Her flattering chatter is really only addressed to your barn. Trust a woman, trust a thief!' It is not very clear whether the picturesque expression 'bedizened rump' relates to a wife or a harlot. Émile Mireaux (*La Vie quotidienne au temps d'Homère*, Hachette, p. 227) concludes that the latter is meant. But I myself would connect this passage with those about marriage. An uncouth, miserly peasant would fear more than anything else having to feed a useless mouth, which would be the case with a frivolous and lazy wife, even if the mouth—not to mention rumps!—were a pretty one. In the *Clouds* of Aristophanes, for instance (46–52), the rough and ready Strepsiades, also a peasant, complains that he has married 'a city madam, one of the fine finicking sort ... stinking of perfume, saffron, lewd kisses, waste of money, gluttony and Aphrodite'.

Hesiod is also guided by the same principle of economy when he writes: 'Get yourself first of all a house, a woman and a working ox. Buy the woman, don't marry her. Then you can make her follow the plough if necessary.' (*Works and Days*, 405–6.) In lines 376–7 he has already hoped: 'May you have no more than one son to look after his father's estate. For so it is that wealth accumulates in dwellings. And may you die at a ripe age, leaving your son to succeed you.'

Yet this hard-working country fellow, so avaricious and

devoted to the soil, was not insensitive to the beauty and grace of youth. Otherwise he would not have been a Greek. In a splendid description of winter he observes: 'Nor does the chill breath of Boreas pierce the delicate flesh of the girl who stays indoors at her loving mother's side, still ignorant of the works of golden Aphrodite. She bathes her young form and anoints it with rich unguents before going to lie down at the further end of her dwelling.' (520–3.)

Was hatred of women partly responsible for the rise of pederasty or was it homosexuality itself that made men despise the other sex? The question is difficult to answer. In any case the pederast, unless bisexual, is usually a misogynist. For example, in the *Erotikos* of Plutarch (751 B and 752 C) Protogenes and Pisias, both champions of homosexuality, discuss women and their lovers in these terms:

'The enfeebling and home-keeping type of love, addicted to the robes and beds of women, always on the prowl for pleasures unworthy of a man, indulged in without friendship or zest, should be proscribed. . . . Men who confess that they are permanently coupled, like dogs, to their females, have actually dared to transport the god Eros from the gymnasia and the meeting-places of philosophers to dens of razors'—in ancient Greece this implement, as already noted, was associated with the feminine, not the masculine, toilet—'rouge and all the other aids to witchcraft used by shameless women.'

It appears then, not that Hesiod himself was a pederast, for there is no evidence of any such thing, but that his misogyny, if common in his environment, signified the existence or imminence of a separation of the sexes in Greek society. It would follow that genuine affection could not accompany marriage, with the result that pederasty became an institution.

Unfortunately we know very little about Greek customs in the seventh and sixth centuries B.C., apart from the extremely valuable and mutually complementary evidence of the poems of Sappho and Theognis, mentioned in the previous chapter, and some verses by Solon and Anacreon which clearly prove the spread of homosexuality.

Herodotus (VI, 126–30) tells a long story about Cleisthenes, the tyrant of Sicyon at the beginning of the sixth century. The monarch wished to arrange the marriage of his daughter Agariste. After his victory at the Olympic Games he ordered a herald to proclaim that 'any Greek who considered himself a suitable applicant for the girl's hand should present himself at Sicyon within a period of sixty days.' Suitors arrived from all the regions of Greece and even from Italy and Ionia. From Athens came Megacles, a member of the Alcmaeonid family, and the rich young nobleman Hippocleides. Cleisthenes kept all the suitors at his Court for a whole year, in order to study them at his leisure. On the day appointed for the tyrant's final choice and the wedding banquet to follow, the candidates continued to compete with one another in singing verses, playing musical instruments and uttering witty sallies. Hippocleides actually mounted a table and began dancing on his hands, with his legs in the air. Cleisthenes had till then favoured him, in secret, above all the rest. But the young Athenian's antics caused him to exclaim: 'Hippocleides, you have danced away your marriage.' The tyrant then chose the other Athenian, Megacles, who duly married Agariste and by her became the father of Cleisthenes the Reformer and thus the ancestor, in the female line, of Pericles.

We need not take this gossip by the worthy Herodotus too literally. But on the assumption that the various incidents and embellishments of the tale are engrafted on a core of historic truth we may deduce that the ancient customs of marriages at Court had survived from Homer's time into the Greek 'Middle Ages'. (See Chapter 1.)

Herodotus also recounts (VI, 61–3) the curious manner in which Ariston, King of Sparta, married a third wife after two previous marriages which proved barren. His closest friend Agetus had married the best-looking woman in the country.

'Ariston fell violently in love with her. So he conceived the following plan. He invited Agetus to choose anything he liked in the palace and take it as a gift, on condition that Agetus offered him the same privilege. Agetus was not anxious about his wife, since he knew that Ariston was already married. So he agreed to the proposal. Both parties took an oath to abide by the agreement. Ariston then gave Agetus the item which his friend selected among the royal treasures. But when the king's turn came he carried off the other's wife. Agetus protested that he would have agreed to anything but that. Nevertheless, being bound by his oath, he consented to the abduction. So it was that Ariston married a third wife after he had dismissed his second.'

This remarkable application of the principle already mentioned, to the effect that among friends all is held in common, was not unique at Sparta, as we shall soon see.

Another anecdote by Herodotus (VI, 122) reports singular conduct on the part of an Athenian of the sixth century B.C.

'He dealt with his three daughters as follows. As soon as they were of an age to marry he endowed them most generously and then let each of them choose any Athenian she pleased as a husband, whereupon he gave her in marriage to the man she had selected.'

Herodotus lived in the fifth century. He apparently approves of the paternal attitude described. But he also seems to regard it as altogether exceptional.

The fact is that in the fifth century the normal rule was that formulated by a late minor poet, Naumachios:

'Take as husband the man your parents prefer.'

No alternative was generally practicable. For in classical Greece neither unmarried nor married women were regarded as legally entitled to act independently. They remained subject all their lives to the authority of a male citizen, usually their father or husband, but in the absence of such persons a masculine tutor or near relative. In Periclean Athens women who had been born free had no more political or legal rights than slaves. Their position contrasted strikingly with that of women under the Minoan and Achaean civilisations, who were not, indeed, considered the equals of men but did apparently enjoy, by custom rather than by law, much more liberty than they would have been allowed at Athens.

Persons thus condemned to a perpetual legal minority, however old they might be, could hardly expect to be permitted, in default of any other rights, the right to love, in other words free choice of the man with whom they would have to live.

It is true that, even in classical times, custom modified to some slight extent the inhuman restrictions to which freeborn Greek women were subjected. A wife trusted by her husband was given complete charge of her domestic affairs. If the family employed slaves she acted as their mistress. Her husband, in any case, would usually be too busy elsewhere to argue with her about the management of his household, where her status resembled that of a Cabinet Minister. To her would preferably be delegated responsibility for the proper conduct of all domestic affairs. For the husband would be incessantly occupied by professional or public business, since Athenian citizens, especially those resident in the capital, gave a very great deal of their time to attendance at the Assembly and in the courts of law. There were also numerous State duties which they might be called upon to perform. Legally, however, the wife depended entirely on her husband and he was entitled to withdraw at any moment such confidence as he reposed in her.

But in Lacedaemonia and no doubt in other Dorian

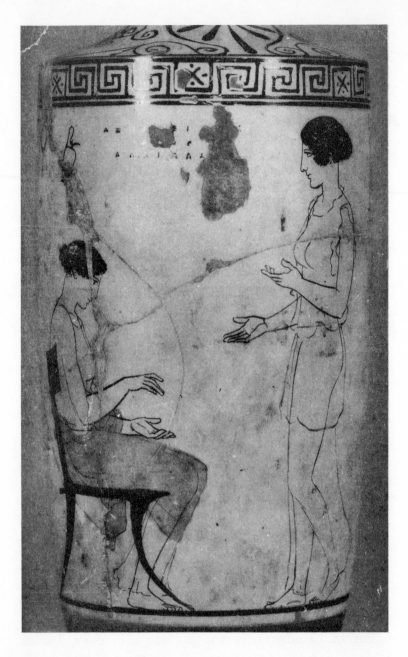

Woman and Servant. Athenian funerary lekythos, painted in colors on a white ground, c. 440 B.C. *Courtesy Museum of Fine Arts, Boston.*

settlements girls retained some freedom of movement throughout the classical period. It is rather surprising to find that in this particular connection the sternly disciplined Spartans were more indulgent than the liberally minded Athenians. But attention to eugenics was a long-established tradition on the banks of the Eurotas. This preoccupation caused Spartans to equate the physical training of girls with that of boys. Consequently, their young women could be seen in short tunics, 'showing their thighs' and

'parading out of doors with bands of youths,
legs bare, their garments floating in the breeze.'

These lines come from the *Andromache* of Euripides (597 *sqq.*), who was scandalised by such proceedings just because he was an Athenian. In his own native land virgins led very different lives, confined in the gynecea. At most they would occasionally appear in the interior courtyard of the family dwelling. For they had to remain in seclusion even from the eyes of their own male relatives, except at festivals.

Yet, athletic as Spartan girls might be, they had no more opportunity than those of Athens to obtain any mental education worth the name. In classical times they knew nothing but what they had learned from their mother, a grandmother or a servant. It amounted to very little, consisting mainly of domestic tasks, especially the spinning and weaving of wool, together with the rudiments of reading and calculating, and sometimes of music and the dance. Choruses of Spartan girls were very highly esteemed. But female children never went to school like the boys. Nowhere in classical Greece, so far as is known, did any institution exist comparable with that maintained by Sappho in Lesbos at the beginning of the sixth century.

Such serious shortcomings in the education of young women unquestionably account for the general lack of spiritual and intellectual contact between husband and wife.

There is not much to be made of girlish babble, however incessant!

According to Plutarch in his life of Lycurgus (15, 1, 2) the Spartan lawgiver relied on the sight of half-dressed virgins to persuade young men to marry.

'These processions of girls, their nude limbs and the contests in which they engaged in the presence of the youths encouraged them to wed. For, as Plato has it, they were swept away by the constraining power of love, which exceeds that of geometry.'

But in this case, perhaps, the sex instinct rather than love might have been invoked. For these young Lacedaemonians, destined to be the mothers of future warriors, were bred and put on show like so many sturdy fillies.

Even stranger measures were taken at Sparta to reduce male celibacy. Hardened bachelors were subjected to all kinds of petty persecution. For example, 'the magistrates would force them to strip naked in the depth of winter and march round the main square of the town, singing a ditty which had been written to ridicule them and proclaiming that they were justly punished for having broken the law'. No doubt elderly spinsters, who were certainly permitted, like the rest of the population, to watch this performance, thoroughly enjoyed it!

At Athens celibacy was not prohibited officially. But it was equally uncongenial to the custom of the country. The desire to have at least one son led most young men to marry sooner or later. Only those whose elder brothers were already fathers could remain bachelors without public censure.

Spartan boys and girls knew each other quite well and had little to learn about their respective anatomies before marriage. But this was not at all the case in Athens and most other Greek cities.

In Xenophon's *Oeconomics*, Ischomachus remarks of his young wife:

'What could she have known, Socrates, when I married

her? She was not yet fifteen. She had always been strictly supervised. She had only been allowed to see and hear what was absolutely essential and to put as few questions as possible.'

Such was, in fact, the ideal of respectability for girls of good family. It is probable, however, that among the masses of the people the rules were less scrupulously observed. For restricted accommodation must often have rendered them impossible to keep.

In the same work Ischomachus addresses his wife herself in these terms:

'Do you understand now why I married you and why your parents consented to our union? We could easily have found someone else to share my bed. I'm sure you realise that perfectly well. But after thinking it over, I in my own interests and your parents in yours, and reviewing all the possible candidates for our household management and the care of our children, I selected you and your parents myself, no doubt from a good many others.'

The phrasing is remarkably cool and certainly has nothing of a lover's declaration about it. L. Dugas has noted that in this view of marriage 'economic considerations are more important than moral. . . . Xenophon is telling his readers how to get rich. If family life is to prosper, the wife must be able to control it. Ischomachus and his wife are simply partners in a farming business, which they shrewdly manage together in their common interests. In their case household management takes the place of domestic virtue and appears in its guise. Xenophon's *Oeconomics* is just what its title proclaims.' (*L'amitié antique*, etc., Paris, Alcan, 1894, p. 81). Even today people will say, 'I have a farm, and a farmer must have a wife. So I'm getting married.'

Many Athenians in fact decided to marry, not only in order to obtain a son, but also to make sure of a good housewife.

It would of course be absurd to maintain that in the fifth

century no Athenian really loved his wife. For a marriage concluded on such practical grounds as the founding of a family and the promotion of legitimate business interests may very well lead to true and deep affection between a married couple.

In point of fact, a passage may be unearthed in Xenophon's *Symposium* (8, 3) which proves the existence of at least one such loving pair. 'Niceratus, they tell me, said Socrates, is in love with his wife and she is in love with him.'

It is also rather remarkable to find that Euripides, whose hatred of women sometimes echoes that of Hesiod, put on the stage three sublime examples of death-defying conjugal devotion, those of Alcestis, Laodamia and Evadne. (See Chapter 2.) These characters however, were heroines, not heroes. The somewhat cold speeches of Admetus, when he is about to profit from the self-sacrifice of his wife Alcestis, indicate gratitude and complacent egoism rather than passionate love. The tragedy of *Protesilaus* is lost. But this hero may perhaps have been represented as the equal in emotional depth of his wife Laodamia.

A marriage between freeborn Athenian citizens included a ceremony more formal than ordinary betrothal. It was called 'Pledging' and consisted in essence of an oral but binding agreement, undertaken before witnesses, between two persons, the bridegroom and the girl's *kyrios*, i.e. her father if alive or if deceased her guardian. They shook hands and uttered certain stereotyped phrases, no doubt reflected accurately enough in the following passage from a play by Menander.

PATAICUS. I give you this girl that she may bear legitimate children.
POLEMON. I receive her.
PATAICUS. I add a dowry of three talents.
POLEMON. I receive it likewise, with pleasure.

(*The Crop-haired Woman*, 435.)

Exactly the same formula is pronounced in Menander's *Curmudgeon* (842-4), recently published by V. Martin from a papyrus text. The piece ends with the marriage of Sostratus to the half-sister of Gorgias and the latter's wedding to the sister of Sostratus. Both ceremonies are concluded without either bride having been consulted or even mentioned by name.

It is not clear whether the brief ceremony of 'Pledging' was attended by the future wife. It is certain, however, that if so she took no active part in the proceedings and was not required to give her consent.

If the bridegroom had attained his legal majority he did not have to be represented by his father and attended the 'Pledging' in person. But he would normally, no doubt, have obtained his father's approval beforehand. In fact, he usually took the latter's advice in selecting a wife. In the oration of Demosthenes *Against Boeotus* (11, 12-13) one of the litigants states:

'When I had reached the age of eighteen my father insisted on my marrying the daughter of Euphemus. He wanted to see that I had children. I considered that I was bound to do whatever he pleased. So I obeyed him and that was how I got married.'

It is evident that in such cases the father chose a wife for his son, either among his own relatives or elsewhere, with a view to establishing or reinforcing certain connections, being guided above all by considerations of material advantage and social expediency.

As we have seen, Hesiod apparently recommended marrying a neighbour. But the phrase could also mean, marry a girl of the same sort as yourself, neither above nor below you. In the *Clouds* of Aristophanes reference is made to an ill-assorted couple, the farmer Strepsiades and his 'city madam', whom he so bitterly regretted marrying.

'Oh, that match-maker!' he exclaims. 'Would she had come to a bad end before she worked me up into marrying that mother of yours ... that niece of Megacles the son of Megacles, that fine city-bred lady, me a simple country-man!'

The consequence was that Strepsiades was no longer master in his own house and could not even give his son the name he had chosen. It appears, then, that some Athenian women managed to acquire such influence over their husbands that they led them, as we should say nowadays, 'by the nose'. But we might have guessed it even without the testimony of Aristophanes. For similar situations have arisen at all times and in all countries.

Pittacus of Mytilene, one of the Seven Sages of Greece, illustrated this golden rule of Hesiod's in graphic fashion. According to Callimachus (Epigram I) he had been asked whether it would be better to marry a girl equal to the enquirer by birth and fortune or a social superior. Pittacus pointed with his staff to some children who were spinning tops. 'They'll give you the answer', he said. The children were continually calling out: 'Stick to your own top!' This oracle from the playground was at once understood by the perplexed young man. He went off and married the girl who belonged to his own class.

There is no need in these pages to describe the marriage ceremony in detail. As in the Homeric age it consisted essentially in the solemn transfer of the bride from her father's house to that of her future husband. We may note, however, that at Athens none of the customary rites appears to have stressed the intimate union of the pair. All the proceedings seem rather to have envisaged the material prosperity of the family and the fertility of the wife. The bride, on arrival at her future home, ate a piece of cake and an apple. But she did not offer any of the food to the bride-groom. Mutual affection between the couple was not emphasised in any way.

At Sparta, as one might expect, marriage itself was subject to the laws of eugenics. Plutarch's life of Lycurgus (15) states:

'Marriage at Sparta was a process of abduction. Wives had to be full grown, never very young'—the Greeks never married girls below the age of puberty, as the Romans did—'The bride, once carried off, was handed over to a special female attendant, who cut her hair short, dressed her up in a man's tunic and shoes and laid her on a straw mattress, where she was left alone in the dark. The bridegroom dined in the usual way with his friends. Then he visited the bride, removed her belt and carried her to a bed. After a short time with her he rejoined his companions in the dormitory for men of his own age. He continued always to act in this way, spending both day and night in male company and only going in secret, with every precaution, to join his wife. He would have been ashamed to be caught doing so by anyone in the house. . . . These habits were kept up for such a long time that sometimes a husband had children without ever having seen his wife by daylight.'

Oddly enough, such marriages, arranged almost entirely for purposes of procreation, rarely resulted in a large family. For in the first place the husband found no difficulty in satisfying his sexual instincts elsewhere, and secondly selfishness or poverty prevented numbers of parents from having many children. Hesiod's advice to have only one son was often taken.

It was only in the rather exceptional case of a wife whose father had died without male heirs that Solon enjoined the husband 'to have intercourse with her at least three times a month', the object being to bring about as soon as possible the birth of a son to inherit the family property. Plutarch is certainly mistaken when he writes in the *Erotikos* (769 A) that 'in this decree Solon's intention was to give the marriage a new lease of life to some extent by invigorating it through such tender attentions'. For he here invests the lawgiver with his own idea of conjugal affection.

Menander expressed a widespread sentiment in the sentence: 'No one is so wretched as a father, except another father who has more children than he.' But as a rule he would prefer boys to girls. Another comic poet remarks: 'One always brings up a son, even if one is poor. But daughters are abandoned, even if the father is rich.' The procedure of abandonment was to place the new-born infant in a clay vessel of some kind and leave it without food in some deserted region. It was unfortunately a common practice, like abortion. Both customs were sanctioned by law and habit, so long as the father concerned had no objection.

A husband always had the right to repudiate his wife, even without showing cause. But a wife could not obtain a divorce except under extreme provocation. Mere adultery by the husband, however open and recognised by public opinion, could not be cited by the wife as grounds for a separation. On the other hand, adultery by the wife rendered her repudiation obligatory. Refusal to dismiss her entailed the loss of civil rights by the husband.

Despite this rigorous legislation some Athenian and Spartan wives did not hesitate to deceive their husbands. At Athens the speech composed by Lysias *On the Murder of Eratosthenes* is full of details of great interest for the historian of morals. The Athenian Euphiletus had married a model wife, 'a clever and thrifty manager, perfect mistress of her household'. Her husband was delighted with her. But at the funeral of his mother, an occasion which was one of the few on which Athenian women left their houses, the wife of Euphiletus was seen by Eratosthenes, who fell in love with her. Shortly afterwards, by bribing a servant, he contrived to enter the house of Euphiletus by night. The latter happened to be sleeping on the first floor in order to leave his wife, who was suckling a child, more convenient accommodation for this purpose in the ground-floor apartments. Eratosthenes found his way there without arousing the husband. But another married woman, also the mistress of Eratosthenes, told Euphiletus what had occurred. He cross-examined his female staff and found that he had in fact been deceived. Thereupon he confided in certain friends and arranged to be warned next time Eratosthenes came to see his wife. When the seducer arrived Euphiletus, as the law permitted, killed him.

In the winter of 413–12 Alcibiades was living at Sparta, having been exiled from Athens. The Lacedaemonian king, Agis, was in the field with his army, at Deceleia in Attica.

'During an earthquake Alcibiades was seen coming out of the apartment of Timaea, the king's wife. It was an obvious case of adultery, which soon became known at Sparta and in Athens, where unmistakable allusions to it were made by the comic poets. The information also probably reached Deceleia, where no doubt the unfortunate husband learned of the affair.' (Jean Hatzfeld, *Alcibiade*, Presses Universitaires, 2e ed., pp. 217–18.) Nine months later, in the autumn of 412, Timaea gave birth to a child, named Leotychidas. But in private, while fondling the infant, she called it by the name of its real father, Alcibiades.

At Sparta, however, married women often embarked on love-affairs with their husbands' consent, if we are to believe Plutarch (*Lycurgus*, 15, 11–15).

'Lycurgus also desired to eliminate jealousy. . . . He made it lawful for the elderly husband of a young wife to allow her the company of a young man of good birth whom he himself esteemed and liked and to authorise intercourse between them, so as to obtain a well-connected son, whom he would then treat as his own. Furthermore, a man of high reputation who admired the prolific and respectable wife of another man could request the loan of her person, as of a fertile piece of land, for the production by himself of fine children with good blood in them. . . .' This decree may have some bearing on the story of Ariston and Agetus told above. Plutarch continues: 'Lycurgus used to say that other lawgivers had bitches and mares coupled with male animals of good stock, lent by their owners free of charge or for a certain fee. He saw no reason why women, on the contrary, should be kept under lock and key, prevented from having children by anyone but their husbands, though the latter might be imbeciles, senile or diseased.'

If relations between the sexes should really be governed by eugenic considerations alone, such selfishness would be unjustifiable. Germany under Hitler deliberately followed the example of Sparta. Girls of pure Aryan race were encouraged to produce sons for the fatherland out of wedlock. But long before that time Plato, too, was intelligibly enough dazzled by the 'Spartan mirage' when he advocated in the *Republic* that in the ideal city women should be held in common, at any rate among the military caste.

In the Greek view neither menstruation nor the sexual intercourse itself of a married couple entailed any defilement requiring subsequent purification on religious grounds.

'Yet, since any physical uncleanness contaminates the gods, a Greek husband and wife were forbidden to embrace in a shrine. If Myrrhina had accepted the suggestion of Cinesias to meet even in a grotto dedicated to Pan, she could not have returned to the Acropolis without washing in the Clepsydra fountain.' (Louis Moulinier, *Le Pur et l'Impur dans la pensée des Grecs*, Klincksieck, 1952, pp. 64–5. The reference is to the *Lysistrata* of Aristophanes, 912–13.)

At Athens marriage did not release women from their sedentary and confined existence. The gynecea were not actually bolted and barred. Nor were the doors locked except at night. But custom ensured that women should stay at home. 'A respectable wife', Menander observes, 'ought to keep indoors. Only good-for-nothing women frequent the street.' It was as a rule the men or slaves who did the necessary daily marketing. Occasionally, however, a married woman might have to buy something for herself, such as a garment or a pair of shoes. She would then have to be accompanied on the unavoidable expedition by a female attendant.

'A brief exposition of the rules of feminine respectability, attributed to Phyntis, a female philosopher of the Pythagorean school, allows only three pretexts for a decent woman to leave her house. She may participate in a festival, make purchases or fulfil religious duties.' (H. Jeanmaire, *Dionysos*, Payot, 1951, p. 168.)

It is most important in the present connection to remember that at Athens in the fifth century wives hardly ever saw their husbands except in the bedchamber. The couple rarely ate together, unless a family reunion was in progress. The Lacedaemonian practice of a common table was replaced at Athens by meals in the 'club' (*thiasos*) and among gatherings of friends. The women usually ate in the gynecea, as they did at Miletus, where Herodotus tells us (I, 146) that they 'never took their meals with their husbands'. In Plato's *Laches* (179 b), Lysimachus, who has a great friend named Melesias, says: 'Melesias and I always eat together and our sons are at table with us.' When an Athenian invited friends to visit him, his wife did not appear at the party. Nor did she accompany him when he was himself invited elsewhere.

The brief exchange between Socrates and Critobulus in Xenophon's *Oeconomics* seems to me highly significant in this respect:

SOCRATES. Well, Critobulus, we're all friends here and you positively must tell us the whole truth. Are there any people you talk to less than you do to your wife?
CRITOBULUS. Possibly. But if so, very few indeed.

In such circumstances it is hardly credible that in classical times Athenian married couples habitually shared thoughts and feelings in any real sense or based their mutual affection on any such reciprocity. There may have been a good many exceptions, like that of Niceratus, who is said by Xenophen to have been in love with his wife. But there cannot have been much communication of ideas between them or much genuine devotion.

Accordingly, Athenians fell easy victims to the charms of women who happened also to be knowledgeable. But they would nearly always be foreigners. Pericles, for instance, married to one of his relatives and the father of two sons by her, dismissed his wife and took Aspasia to live with him. She was a woman of intelligence and in every respect remarkable. Socrates had the highest opinion of her. But she had been born at Miletus in Ionia. So Pericles could not marry her. He was obliged to make her his concubine. It seems that they lived happily together until he died of the plague in 429. But the comic poets took a violent dislike to Aspasia, going as far as to insinuate that she was a harlot and ran a brothel. Marie Delcourt (*Pericles*, Gallimard, 1939, p. 77) observes:

'No one would have objected if Pericles had been fond of young men or cruel to his first wife. But people were scandalised to find that he considered her successor a human being, keeping her in his own apartments instead of shutting her up in the gynecea and asking his friends to bring their wives to meet her. Such behaviour was judged too astonishing to be natural and Aspasia herself too brilliant to be respectable.'

This feminine comment implies severe censure, not to be wondered at, of Athenian habits. But it is not, in fact, so very long since modern man came to a full realisation that 'women, too, are individuals'.

Two British scholars, however (A. W. Gomme, *Essays on Greek History and Literature*, Oxford, Blackwell, 1937, pp. 89–115, and H. D. F. Kitto, *The Greeks*, Pelican Books, 1951, pp. 219–36), believe that Athenian women enjoyed a great deal more liberty and esteem than has been admitted above.

For most of the fifth century family life remained stable at Athens. But the Peloponnesian War, which lasted thirty years and was fought out with terrible ferocity, introduced great changes into the habits of the people. The devastating plague of 429, which killed Pericles, was one of the results of the war. Thucydides (II, 53) thus describes the effects of this epidemic on public morals:

'The rapid changes of fortune that occurred, when the rich died suddenly and the poverty-stricken inherited their estates, encouraged the citizens to give themselves up openly to pleasures which they would formerly have concealed. Instantly available enjoyment was preferred, in the belief that sensuality was all that mattered, since property and life itself were so ephemeral.'

The endless fighting kept the men continuously absent from their homes, including the matrimonial couch, that 'unique meeting-place' of a married couple. Many women found themselves obliged to take over the direction of family affairs from their husbands. Their manners, accordingly, like those of the women of Sparta, became more free and easy. They stayed at home less. So many scandals arose in consequence of this behaviour that in the fourth century a special magistrate was appointed to supervise female conduct.

Two comedies by Aristophanes, the *Lysistrata* of 411 and the *Ecclesiazusae* of 392, might even suggest the beginnings of a movement for feminine emancipation at Athens. The remarkable expedient devised by women, in the *Lysistrata*, to force their husbands to put an end to the war is well known. They resolved that, when the latter came home for their brief periods of 'leave', sexual intercourse should be denied them so long as peace had not been concluded. It is possible that some Athenian wives had become convinced that a policy directed solely by men was bringing the city to ruin. They may have thought that matters were likely to improve if they themselves were allowed to have a say in the management of affairs and could advise their husbands. But these plays by Aristophanes amount to little more than jocose and spirited sallies, outbursts of his exuberant imagination. It would be very rash to take them seriously. Nevertheless, the very choice of such subjects seems to me a sign of the times. For much other evidence confirms the supposition that the

Athenian woman of the fourth century was starting to free herself a little from the almost suffocating grip of the conventions
from which her mother and grandmother had suffered.

Socrates, though he had little esteem for his wife Xanthippe, boldly committed himself to what was then a
paradox, viz., the equality of the sexes. In Xenophon's
Symposium (2) he exclaims, in admiration of the skill of a
female dancer, 'Women are by no means inferior to men.
All they need is a little more physical strength and energy of
mind.' Such, too, must have been Plato's opinion. For,
according to Diogenes Laertius, he admitted at least two
women to the Academy, though it is true that they were
foreigners. One came from Mantinea in Arcadia, being thus a
compatriot of the priestess Diotima, who appears in his
Symposium. The other had been born at Phlya in Argolis.

As for the men of the fourth century, more and more of
them were following the example of Pericles in the preceding
age. They acquired concubines, but did not always consider
it necessary, as he had, to repudiate their legitimate wives for
that reason. It was a fourth-, not a fifth-century lawyer who
declared in open court, as if it were a matter of course:

'We resort to courtesans for our pleasures, keep concubines
to look after our daily needs and marry wives to give us
legitimate children and be the faithful guardians of our
domestic hearths.' (Pseudo-Demosthenes, *Against Neasera*,
122.)

The concubines might be either lower-class Athenians,
slaves or freeborn foreigners. It is rather doubtful, to judge
from the speeches we have relating to them, whether they had
any legal rights or a recognised social position. But in
practice, if not in law, they seem to have enjoyed considerable
freedom.

The passage just quoted from an address in court indicates
that the legitimate wife was still regarded simply as a mother
and protectress of the hearth. This idea may be noted as a
constant of the Greek social scene. Yet we have good reason

to suppose that genuine affection between men and women and conjugal love in particular became less rare in the fourth century.

Plato never married. He may have been influenced in this decision by the unhappy matrimonial experiences of Socrates. But Plato's disciple Aristotle had a wife named Pythias, a niece of his friend Hermias, tyrant of Atarneus. The philosopher got on very well with her. He frequently notes, for example in the *Nicomachean Ethics* (VIII, 12), his view that marriage should not be a mere association for the purpose of perpetuating the species but an alliance of two reciprocally affectionate and tender persons which may perfectly well meet every moral need of humanity. Here, too, a sign of the times may be discerned.

But the most important proofs of this evolution of manners are furnished by the history of art and in literature by the New Comedy.

The testimony of art is necessarily indirect. But when added to other evidence it is no less characteristic. The sculpture and pottery of the sixth and fifth centuries seldom displayed the female nude. But undraped male athletes and youths occur with almost excessive frequency, as in the Discobulus of Myron, the Doryphorus and Diadumenus of Polycleitus and on vases, among many other handsome lads, the Ganymede with a Cock.

In the fourth century, no doubt, as Jean Charbonneaux states (*La Sculpture grecque classique*, Cluny, 1943, t. II, pp. 79 and 102–3): 'The female nude was no novelty in Greek art before Praxiteles. It remained rare, however, during the sixth and fifth centuries, especially in sculpture. The fact is all the more striking in view of the extraordinary frequency of the male nude. . . . The moral emancipation of Greek women naturally brought with it the discovery of feminine physical charm and of a beauty hitherto overshadowed by the splendours of the masculine form.' It may not perhaps be going too far to suggest that this apotheosis of the male nude

Discobolo of Myron, c. 450 B.C. National Museum, Rome. *Bettmann Archive.*

Terracotta statuette after the Diadumenus of Polycleitus. Probably found at Smyrna. *The Metropolitan Museum of Art, Fletcher Fund, 1932.*

coincided with the development of pederasty, while the new worship of the female figure marked the return of many Greeks to heterosexuality.

The undraped Aphrodite of Scopas, for example, of which the Capitoline Venus is possibly a copy, already shows 'a kind of delight in the analysis of feminine anatomy'. But Aphrodite in all her glory was first unveiled by Praxiteles in a large number of statues, that of Cnidos being the most famous. In the Hellenistic age very many figures of Eros, Aphrodite and Hermaphrodite, in the so-called 'erotic' style, were produced.

Similarly, in vase-painting the legends about Eros and Aphrodite, together with those of Dionysus, the effeminate god of intoxication and ecstasy, were more and more often illustrated during the fourth century. The subjects included representations of Silenus pursuing nymphs, Ariadne lying asleep and carried off by Dionysus, the lascivious frolics of satyrs and maenads, women dancers, players both male and female of the oboe and tambourine, Thetis being chased by Peleus, the judgment of Paris in the beauty competition between the three goddesses, Paris with Helen, and nude women at their toilets in the gynecea.

In the fourth century, therefore, feminine grace and beauty acquired a degree of appreciation in Greek art which far exceeded that accorded them in former times.

The evidence of the New Comedy of Menander, born in 342 B.C., is naturally of a more direct character, since it appears in written form.

Although conjugal affection certainly existed in the fifth century, it was hardly ever mentioned, least of all the love of a husband for a wife, which it was probably considered vulgar to talk about. On the other hand, no secret whatever is made of it in the quite numerous and important fragments of Menander's plays which have survived on papyrus. In *The Arbitration*, for instance, Charisius and Pamphyle have been married for five months and are still very fond of each

Satyr and Bacchic Dancers Moving to Sound of Double Aulos Played by Young Girl. Terracotta relief from Myrina. *Bettmann Archive.*

other. But this young woman had been ravished shortly before her marriage by an unknown man who had forced himself upon her by night during the Tauropolia festival. Her husband was not aware of this circumstance. But on his return from a journey he learnt from a slave that his wife had given birth to a son in his absence. As the infant could not have been conceived in wedlock, Charisius felt obliged to leave Pamphyle. Yet he remained passionately in love with her. To drown his sorrow he began to lead a life of revelry and debauch with a woman lute-player named Habrotonon. By an extraordinary coincidence it turned out that the unknown nocturnal ravisher of Pamphyle had been no other than Charisius himself. Thus the child was his after all. The whole comedy is concerned with the elaborate complication and unravelling of this situation, leading up to the final reconciliation of the young couple. As soon as Charisius learns the truth he exclaims: 'You give me wings of delight!' He has never ceased to love his wife in spite of his terrible suspicion of her, while she on her side has been the most tender and faithful companion that a man could desire, in spite of her involuntary misadventure.

Only a few months ago an almost complete comedy by Menander was discovered. It is called *The Curmudgeon* and was first published, from a papyrus, by Professor Victor Martin of Geneva. In this piece Sostratus, a rich young man of good family, falls madly in love with a girl he sees crowning statuettes of nymphs at the entrance to a grotto dedicated to Pan. He determines to marry her. But first he must find her father and obtain his consent.

'I've seen a girl of the most perfect beauty and I've fallen in love with her. If that's a crime, well, I'm a criminal. But where's the harm in it? I haven't come here to get hold of her but to see her father. I shall tell him that I'm a free-born citizen with plenty of money and am ready to marry her without a dowry and, what's more, to swear that I'll love her for ever.'

The girl herself is poor. But she is chaste and well behaved. The action of the play concentrates upon the manoeuvres to obtain the consent of her father Cnemon to the marriage. For Cnemon is an 'enemy of the human race' and won't talk to anybody.

Menander's comedies repeatedly deal with the problems of marriage and family life. It must be admitted that many of his lines recall the hostility to women characteristic of the preceding centuries. This effect is reinforced by the author's deeply pessimistic general outlook. Yet the treatment of love in his work has quite a different accent from that of Aristophanes in the same connection. This change is probably much more due to social evolution as a whole than to any particular feature of the dramatist's personality.

In his plays and those of the other poets of the New Comedy, which were imitated by the Romans Plautus and Terence, Ph.-E. Legrand, (*Daos*, E. de Boccard, 1910, pp. 184–93 etc.) observes that: 'A wife who deceives her husband scarcely ever appears in the repertory. The lovers are certainly much concerned with physical passion. But they also have more exalted motives for their affection. They are attracted in the first place by good manners and in addition by intelligence, sensitivity, conscientiousness, loyalty and congenial tastes and characters in their partners. They are always ready to accept marriage as the culmination of a love-affair or flirtation. Their mutual affection does not reflect a merely superficial interest but stems from a deliberate study of each other's good qualities.'

The New Comedy unquestionably influenced the lyric and epic poetry of the Alexandrine age. Theocritus, Callimachus, Apollonius of Rhodes and their rivals in the third century dealt again and again with love, usually passionate love between man and woman. But these affairs were rarely of a merely sensual description.

Legrand (*Poésie alexandrine*, Payot, 1924, pp. 64–5) remarks that: 'The Greeks of the third century were much preoccupied with love, all the more so on account of the increased leisure afforded them by the suppression of political activity. One may say that their whole literature is permeated by erotic sentiment. For it is not only the foundation of the personal lyric and an integrating factor of the new material both of this kind and of the dramatic and narrative works of the younger writers. Sexual passion is also introduced as an influence upon the adventures and personalities already familiar from the productions of former authors.'

The case of Achilles, the greatest of the Homeric heroes, is the most illuminating example of social and literary evolution among the Greeks. It is true that in the *Iliad* he regrets the departure of Briseis. But his deepest love is for Patroclus and it remains chaste. Male friendship has never been better depicted. But in the *Myrmidons* of Aeschylus, as we noted in Chapter 3, Achilles and Patroclus have become lovers, owing to the prevalent cult of homosexuality at the time when the tragedy was written. For the Alexandrine poets, however, Achilles was above all the seducer of Deidamia, the lover of Briseis and Polyxena, the chivalrous admirer of Penthesilea and the fascinating commander of hostile troops to whom the Lesbian Peisidice betrayed her native land.

Even the bestial Polyphemus, the Cyclops of the *Odyssey*, ogre and cannibal, falls in with the fashion of the day and sighs for Galatea in the Idyll of Theocritus named after him.

'White Galatea, why dost thou repulse my love? O, thou art whiter to see than curdled milk, more delicate than the lamb, more nimble than the heifer, brighter than a green grape! Why dost thou avoid me?... I have loved thee, maiden, ever since thou camest with thy mother to pluck the flowering hyacinth on the mountainside and I served thee as a guide. I can never cease to love thee. But thou, as Zeus is my witness, takest no thought of me.'

The Alexandrine poets certainly often wrote of love in a conventionally affected style. Their manner is the direct literary ancestor of such a conceit as Racine expressed in his line (from the *Andromache*):

'Burned by a fiercer flame than I did ever kindle!'

Yet at the same time passion is also often phrased by them in authentic and powerful terms, for instance in the story of Acontius and Cydippe from the *Origenes* of Callimachus, a work of which fragments survive, or again in the Idyll of the *Witches* by Theocritus, which recounts the tale of Simaetha and Delphis. (See Chapters 5 and 7.)

Greek epitaphs, incidentally, to the extent that so artificial a type of literature can be of any use to the study of social behaviour, seem to indicate that genuine conjugal affection was quite frequent in the Hellenistic era. But an article on this subject by G. Fohlen in *Les études classiques* for 1954, pp. 150–1, goes too far, in my opinion, when it includes the classical age in the author's conclusions.

In Hellenistic times, however, the greater esteem accorded to women and the love they inspire was naturally accompanied by a return to the ancient tradition of feminine education in vogue, as we have seen, in Lesbos at the period of Sappho. But in the third century such studies do not seem to have taken place in the smouldering, heated atmosphere of female homosexuality characteristic of the former schools.

H.-I. Marrou (*Histoire de l'Éducation dans l'Antiquité*, pp. 66–7) writes:

'So far as can be deduced from documentary evidence feminine education was long eclipsed by the predominantly masculine character of Greek civilisation. It is only much later, hardly before the Hellenistic era, that we have any clear information on the subject. In particular, gatherings were held in which the competitive spirit found expression. They served, like modern examinations, to encourage study. At Pergamum during the Hellenistic and Roman epochs special officers called "Superintendents of the Morals of

Virgins" were charged with the control of mental training for women. Girls, like boys, competed in recitations, music and reading. In other regions, especially in the Aeolian islands, the girls' competitions did not simply copy those of their brothers. The subjects were of specifically feminine interest and corresponded with those of the Sapphic schools. Theophrastus reports that beauty competitions for girls were held, notably in the islands of Lesbos and Tenedos, but also at cities elsewhere. Prizes were given, too, for moral stability (*sophrosyne*) and household management (*oeconomia*).'

Quite a number of female artists and even philosophers were active at this period. Women players of the harp, for instance, gave concerts and many feminine disciples came to hear the lectures of Epicurus. (See Chapters 5 and 6.) It is also significant that the Boeotian poetess Corinna in all probability lived in the Hellenistic age. Accordingly, we need not be surprised to read of 'bluestockings' in that era, though apparently, until then, there had been hardly any Greek women writers at work since the time of Sappho.

A. Aymard (*L'Orient et la Grèce antique*, Presses Universi-taires, 1953, pp. 430–1) sums the situation up as follows. 'Female education was no longer left to the mother, in the closed family circle of the gynecea. Girls went to school and even to the gymnasium, just like their brothers. Sparta was no longer an exception in this respect. Consequently, more freedom was customary among women of the leisured class. Few of these ladies studied abstract theory on a high level. But several wrote poetry. Nor did discussions of literature, philosophy and art remain the privilege of a handful of high-browed courtesans. For the old conventions were breaking down. Women in good society did not yet go out to formal dinner-parties. But they could walk in the streets without attendance and their husbands allowed them to meet males other than their relatives. Manners, too, were becoming more refined. Certain polite gestures, such as kissing the hand, date from this period.'

It is a mistake still too often made to regard the Alexandrine period of Greek civilisation as a decadence. For on the one hand scientific studies in many fields were making unprecedently rapid progress and on the other sexual morality had become on the whole more normal than it had been in the classical epoch. This change of habit favoured the development of an art and a literature in which women and love of them took their natural place, a position which had hardly ever been theirs in Greece, apart from the very special case of Sappho, since the Homeric age.

5

COURTESANS

'There is only one more favour you can still do me. You must come with me to lie in the temple where you have set up my statue with those of Aphrodite and Eros. For how is it possible for us to defile gods whom we ourselves have made?'

ALCIPHRON, Letter from Phryne to Praxiteles.

'WE resort to courtesans for our pleasures. . . .' This phrase by a fourth-century rhetorician was cited in the last chapter. His words prove that paid sexual intercourse was rife among the ancient Greeks. Pederasts were not alone in being able to satisfy their particular tastes without difficulty in the company of outdoor or indoor prostitutes. The heterosexually-minded could also easily find '*hetairai*', obliging 'little friends' who lived by the sale of their bodies.

There were, to begin with, the consecrated courtesans, who were slaves in the service of the goddess of love. For certain religious cults not only tolerated but protected and even organised prostitution, which was considered pleasing to Aphrodite. The female 'acolytes' in question formed a branch, so to speak, of the staff of the temple.

In several cities of Cyprus, such as Paphos and Amathus, this type of prostitution was only practised for a while on certain occasions. Herodotus (I, 199) relates that at Babylon 'every woman, at least once in her life, had to visit a temple of Aphrodite'—he means Ishtar—'and have intercourse with a man unknown to her . . . the ugly ones, whom no one wanted, stayed at the temple for long periods without being able to meet the requirements of the law, sometimes for

three or four years.' He adds: 'In some parts of Cyprus there
is a rather similar custom.' That island, as we know, was pre-
eminently Aphrodite's. She was herself called Cypris, the
Cypriot.

But the true courtesans of this kind were permanently
active, till they died or retired. Their prostitution can
probably be interpreted as a rite of assimilation to the
goddess, an act regarded as conducive to the fertility of all
the women in the region, even of its soil. A similar exercise of
'sympathetic magic' caused the male organ of generation,
the phallus, to be carried in procession at the Dionysian
festivals.

Like Herodotus in his reference to Cypriot customs we
must turn to the East, especially Mesopotamia, to find
parallels to the consecrated courtesans. 'At Uruk in particular,' writes Aymard (op. cit. p. 146), 'consecrated
prostitutes were employed in the temple of Ishtar, called the
"queen of pleasure", to fulfil the rite of homage to the
goddess.' Similar practices characterised the cults of nearly
all the oriental goddesses of Phoenicia, Syria and Asia
Minor. Such deities were identified by the Greeks with
Aphrodite.

In Greece these courtesans were especially numerous at
Corinth. They figured in the ceremonies which took place in
the sacred citadel of Acrocorinthus. According to Strabo
(VIII, 378) the shrine 'was so rich that it acquired more than
a thousand consecrated prostitutes, of whom many were
dedicated to the presiding divinity by private individuals,
both men and women. Consequently, the city attracted
crowds of visitors and grew wealthy. Sailors in particular
were only too ready to spend everything they had in the
place.' For Corinth had two harbours, one on the gulf of that
name and one on the Aegean Sea, with a road between them
along which vessels could be hauled. The crews of countless
ships accordingly visited the town. But the fees charged by
the consecrated prostitutes, as well as by others even more

numerous, were high. Such was the origin of the proverb, *Non licet omnibus adire Corinthum* ('Not everybody can get into Corinth').

Pindar's thirteenth Olympiad was composed in honour of Xenophon of Corinth, who had won the foot-race and the five events of the pentathlon. The pious athlete had not relied entirely on his own strength and skill. He had vowed to dedicate to the Corinthian Aphrodite, if he were successful at Olympia, a contingent of prostitutes. He duly fulfilled his vow. Pindar wrote a second, shorter piece to be recited at the formal presentation of Xenophon's offering to the goddess. (Ed. A. Puech, IV, pp. 188–9.)

'Most hospitable maidens attendant upon Peitho in affluent Corinth'—Peitho, a personification of erotic seduction, was a secondary goddess, often associated with Aphrodite (see Chapter 2)—''tis at your hands the pallid incense smokes upon the altar, while your thoughts often soar aloft to the heavenly mother of loves, Aphrodite ... the goddess permits you, my children, to offer up without reproach upon your pleasant beds the fruits of your delicate youth. For at the bidding of necessity all deeds are well done.... Yet perhaps I shall be blamed by the Masters of the Isthmus'— these were the officers in charge of the Isthmian Games held near Corinth—'for so beginning my honey-sweet song, with mention of harlots.... O sovereign mistress of Cyprus, Xenophon hath led unto thy shrine a band of fifty maidens dedicated to thy service, in token of his joy at the granting of all his prayers.'

When the Persian army of Xerxes threatened Greece, it was the consecrated prostitutes of Corinth who offered up, as priestesses in the temple of Aphrodite, the sacrifices and prayers of the nation in its hour of peril. After Xerxes had been defeated, the citizens of Corinth presented to the shrine a picture of these women in the act of uttering their supplications to the goddess. A quatrain by the great poet Simonides was added:

'Because these women suppliant to the Cyprian stood
for special aid to Corinth, yet for all the Greeks
entreating aid, great Aphrodite would not leave
their citadel to fall, the Persian archers' prey.'

Rome's Capitol was saved by geese, Acrocorinthus by
the prayers of courtesans.

The cult of Aphrodite seemed to be so closely associated
with prostitution that the sophist Euhemerus, who attempted
to 'rationalise' religion by humanising the gods, asserted
that the mother of Eros was not a goddess at all. She had
been, he declared, a courtesan responsible for instituting
prostitution in Cyprus and hence named the 'Cyprian'.

In the central section of the Ludovisi throne one of the
two lateral figures supporting the scene of the birth of
Aphrodite is a charming female nude playing the double
flute. She may well represent a courtesan. For the *hetairai*,
whether consecrated or not, were very often musically gifted.

Ever since archaic times independent prostitutes had been
active in addition to those in the service of religion.

Herodotus (II, 134–5) recounts the edifying tale of
Rhodopis, 'rose-face', a Thracian said to have originally
been a slave, with the fabulist Aesop, in the house of Iadmon,
a Samian. But she very soon acquired a large fortune. On
the principle of 'Unto him that hath shall be given' she was
actually credited with having built one of the Egyptian
pyramids at her own expense.

'Rhodopis', says Herodotus, 'was first brought to Egypt
by Xanthes of Samos. Her intention was to live by the sale of
her favours. She obtained her freedom by paying a large sum
to Charaxos of Mytilene, own brother to the poetess Sappho.
After her release from slavery she stayed in Egypt, where her
abundant charms earned her a great deal of money, quite
enough to satisfy the greed of a courtesan but by no means
adequate for the construction of so large a pyramid. Anyone,
of course, even today, has a perfect right to work out how

Flute-player. Fourth-century relief. Ludovisi Throne. Termi Museum, Rome. *Bettmann Archive.*

much a tenth of her fortune amounted to. But it should not
be regarded as unlimited. Rhodopis wished, in point of fact,
to leave behind her in Greece a monument such as no one
had yet imagined or dedicated in a temple. She meant to
bequeathe it to the shrine at Delphi. Accordingly, she spent
a tithe of her capital on the manufacture of a quantity of iron
spits which could pierce the carcass of an ox. She sent them
to Delphi, where they can still be seen piled up behind
the altar consecrated by the Chians, opposite the temple
itself.'

These 'spits' may have been simply bars of metal. For in
very ancient times the metal bar served the purpose of a coin.
The Greek obol, for instance, is etymologically a spit. In
any case the iron implements in question survived until the
fourth century B.C., when they were used as weapons by the
men of Phocis. Modern research claims that the slab on
which they were piled has been found at Delphi.

There is no evidence, so far as I know, of shrines at Athens
where religious prostitution was practised on the lines in
vogue at Corinth. But Solon is reported to have bought
female slaves to stock the first Athenian brothels. They were
intended as a safety-valve for the erotic ardours of the
younger citizens, which were causing breaches of public
order. Philemon, a poet of the New Comedy, warmly
praised the lawgiver for this measure in a play called *The
Brothers*. We are told that Solon simultaneously decided to
build the first temple in Attica to Aphrodite Pandemos. The
cost was to be met from the profits of the brothel-keepers.
At Athens, then, as elsewhere, religion came to terms with
prostitution and benefited from the arrangement.

The *Deipnosophistai* (Sophists' Banquet) of Athenaeus is the
source of the above information. He goes on to say that in
the age of Themistocles, a century after Solon's time, 'the
Athenians had not yet acquired the habit of getting drunk
and visiting courtesans'. As we have seen, at that period
many Athenians preferred boys. It is certain, however,

that the brothels established by Solon had a good many
competitors later on. For Athenaeus tells us that no Greek
city had as many courtesans as Athens. He means, no
doubt, ordinary prostitutes. For otherwise Corinth would be
pre-eminent.

Habrotonon, the mother of Themistocles himself, is said
to have been a courtesan. In his wild youth, according to
Athenaeus, 'he tied four *hetairai* to a chariot and drove
it through the Pottery Quarter early in the morning, when
the crowds there were thickest'. The author, however,
confesses that his informant, one Idomeneus, did not specify
whether the women had actually been harnessed like horses,
when they would have attracted most attention, or whether
Themistocles simply made them stand beside him in the
vehicle.

The *Memorabilia* of Xenophon (III, 11) has a diverting
account of an innocent visit by Socrates to the fair Theodote.
'There was a beautiful woman named Theodote at Athens.
She was so easy of access that she accorded her favours to
anyone. One of the disciples of Socrates told him that words
could not describe her beauty, that painters used her as a
model and that she displayed to them all that decency
permits a woman to show. "Well, we had better go and see
her," said Socrates. "It's no good our listening to you. For
we can form no idea of what is beyond words." "I'll take
you to her at once," the disciple replied. So they went to her
house, where they found her being studied by a painter.
They examined her at their leisure. Then, when the artist
had finished his work, they engaged her in conversation.'

After an exchange of courtesies Socrates, who had been
admiring the luxury of the apartment and the robes of
Theodote, her mother and their slaves, asked the courtesan:

'"How do you meet your expenses?" "I get friendly with
a man and he is willing to oblige me. That's how I live."
"Well, you certainly seem to make a good thing of it,
Theodote. A host of friends is very much better than flocks of

sheep, many oxen and herds of goats. But if you want a
friend to come flying up to you like a gnat, do you use only
the gifts of fortune to attract him or some trick or other?"
"Oh, I don't know any tricks!"'

Socrates than gives her a few tips for 'hunting friends', a
sport he went in for himself.

'"Instead of using hounds, find someone who'll track down
amorous millionaires for you and steer them into your nets."
"What nets do you think I have, then?" "Only one, but a
good catcher, your beauty, reinforced by your mind, which
inspires you to dart enchanting glances and flattering words."'

At last Theodote asks in her turn:

'"Won't you help me, Socrates, in the chase?" "I will if
you persuade me to do so." "Then come and see me often."
"It'll be difficult for me to find the time, Theodote," he
replies, in ironic reference to his lofty speculations. "My own
affairs and those of the State leave me no leisure. Moreover,
I have certain mistresses who won't leave me alone day or
night. For they have learnt from me how to use love potions
and witchcraft. . . ." "Please lend me a magic bird, then, so
that I can put a spell on you." "But I don't want to be
forced to come to you. I demand, on the contrary, that you
come to see me." "I'll come, Socrates, if you promise to let
me in." "I certainly will, if I haven't got anyone with me
whom I like better than you."'

We shall return later to the subject of erotic witchcraft,
with its love potions and the 'magic bird' alluded to by
Theodote in the above passage.

Alcibiades, a disciple of Socrates, though a restive and
rebellious one, did not limit himself to admiring and chatting
with the *hetairai*. We have already referred to his tastes in
the chapter on homosexuality and also in the last chapter,
when his adultery with the wife of a king of Sparta was
mentioned. Nor can his name be omitted in dealing with the
courtesans of ancient Greece.

When this handsome young man, in Plato's *Symposium*,

turns up at Agathon's banquet at an unseasonable hour, he enters reeling and intoxicated, supported by a female oboe player, unquestionably a courtesan, and some boon companions. He is wearing a kind of wreath on his head, composed of ivy leaves and violets. His wife Hipparete, who was of noble birth, soon wearied of his infidelities and orgies, which took place even in his own house. She filed a petition for divorce with the archon. But Alcibiades, probably because he would have had to return her dowry if she obtained a separation, exercised his prerogative to insist upon her remaining his wife. Finally, after he had been sentenced to death by the Thirty Tyrants and Lysander and was in flight, pursued from one refuge to another by a pack of assassins, the courtesan Timandra alone accompanied him. According to Plutarch (*Alcibiades*, 39), after he had been killed she 'took up his corpse, wrapped it in her own robes and gave him as splendid a funeral as she could afford'.

The same Timandra, so loyal to her lover in misfortune and even after his death, gave birth to the famous courtesan Lais, called the 'Corinthian', though she was born in Sicily.

While Lais was still very young, the celebrated painter Apelles predicted a brilliant future for her. Other artists regularly visited her, as they had Theodote, to copy the wonderful beauty of her bosom.

One of her numerous lovers was the Socratic philosopher Aristippus of Cyrene. Someone who wanted to annoy Lais once told him that she did not love him. 'That doesn't matter to me,' he answered. 'I don't suppose fish or wines love me either. But I take pleasure in both all the same.' The remark was typical of a predecessor of Epicurus, who argued that bodily pleasure had nothing to do with love.

In the *Erotikos* (769 F) Plutarch describes as follows the tragic end of Lais:

'You have heard tell of Lais, who was the theme of poets and so much loved. You know that she inflamed all Greece with desire and that suitors came to woo her from both seas'

—i.e. the Ionian and the Aegean, for she lived in Corinth—
'After falling in love with the Thessalian Hippolochus she
abandoned, as Euripides has it, "Acrocorinthus and the
grey waves that lap it round." Secretly escaping from her
many other lovers and the vast army of courtesans in that
city, she fled, without incurring reproach, to Thessaly. But
the women of that country, being envious and jealous of her
beauty, dragged her to a shrine of Aphrodite, where they
stoned her to death.'

The next most famous of the Greek courtesans was
undoubtedly the Boeotian Phryne, who came from Thespiae.
She became, in particular, the mistress of the great Athenian
sculptor Praxiteles, who use her as a model for his statues of
Aphrodite. He actually erected one of his figures of her
between those of the goddess and Eros in a temple at
Thespiae. (See quotation at the head of this chapter.) It was
said that Phryne's real name was Mnesarete, 'she who
remembers virtue', certainly an odd way of describing a
future courtesan. The word 'phryne', which means 'toad',
is supposed to have been applied to her on account of her
yellowish complexion. But whatever the colour of her skin—
which she may have improved with white lead—she had a
splendid figure. The orator Hyperides, another of her lovers,
once defended her in a court of law, as is well known, on
strange grounds.

G. Colin, in his edition of the works of Hyperides, thus
describes the case:

'One of her lovers, Euthias, quarrelled with her. By way
of revenge he charged her with impiety. He accused her in
particular of having practised shameless debauchery in a
holy place. The crime was serious and might entail the
penalty of death. Hyperides undertook the defence of his
mistress. He made a speech of which only insignificant odds
and ends remain. But ancient writers praise its charm and
ingenuity. Yet it appeared that this piece of eloquence had
not convinced the judges. They seemed about to pronounce

sentence when Hyperides led his client forward and with a
sudden gesture tore the robe from her breast. The sight of her
beauty acted as the most pathetic of perorations. The judges
felt that they could not conscientiously put to death "a
priestess, a servant of Aphrodite". But they subsequently
passed a decree designed to prevent any such surprises in
future. It forbade the presence of an accused person in court
while a verdict was being considered.'

The editor adds: 'Several sculptors and painters have
dramatised the scene. For it provided them with an excellent
opportunity for reviving in marble or on canvas the graces of
the woman who is said to have inspired Praxiteles in the
Cnidian Aphrodite and Apelles in the "Birth of Aphrodite".'
But Colin does not believe the story. He may or may not be
right. Yet, even if untrue, so effective a tale could only have
been invented in Greece. For it is highly significant of the
genuinely religious importance attributed there to physical
beauty. Phryne, as a 'priestess and servant of Aphrodite',
like the consecrated courtesans of Acrocorinthus, was bound
to elicit admiration and respect from the judges. In the same
way Helen, as she passed along the ramparts of Troy, had
aroused the enthusiasm of the Trojan elders. Yet her guilt,
too, was clear. She had even brought much suffering upon
those who watched her. Nevertheless, as Paris had said
(see Chapter 1): 'The enchanting gifts of golden Aphrodite
come from the gods alone and none may of his own will
acquire them.' They might, indeed, be considered the sign
manual of a sort of divine choice. The Stoics, the severest of
the philosophers, affirmed that a handsome boy must
necessarily possess a fine mind, gifted with virtue. Consequently, a woman upon whom Aphrodite had bestowed all
her attractions could scarcely be judged as if she were one
not distinguished by such marks of the favour of heaven.

Hyperides was also the lover of several other courtesans of
less note than Phryne. He kept Myrrhina, one of the most
popular, in his house at Athens, Aristagora at the port of

Piraeus, and Phila on his estate at Eleusis. He must have earned substantial fees by his speeches in court if he could afford to maintain three mistresses at the same time!

Phryne, like Rhodopis before her and perhaps following her example, resolved to leave a memorial of her glory in the temple of the Pythian Apollo at Deplhi. But her bequest took a more personal form than iron spits. We are told that it was a statue 'in gold'—the expression probably means gilded bronze—by her lover Praxiteles. The figure was placed on the top of a tall pillar of Pentelic marble, close to the main altar. This work excited the virtuous indignation of the cynic philosopher Crates, who called it 'a trophy set up to commemorate Greek sensuality'. For it was in fact the custom, when a Greek city won a battle, to present a tithe of the spoil to Delphi. And Phryne, like Rhodopis, had thus dedicated a tithe of the sums extorted from lovers 'vanquished by her beauty'.

Courtesans who gave up their profession to devote themselves to a single supporter, as did Lais when she fell in love with Hippolochus, sometimes proved excellent and loyal companions. The philosopher Aristotle had greatly loved his wife Pythias, by whom he had a daughter. After the former's death he lived with Herpyllis, who is said to have been a prostitute. She presented him with a son to whom he gave the name, as was usual, of his own father, Nicomachus. It was to this son that Aristotle dedicated his great treatise on morals known as the Nicomachean Ethics. The philosopher's will, quoted by Diogenes Laertius, provided most generously for Herpyllis, 'to remember me by', he wrote, 'and in gratitude for the affection she always showed me and the care she took of my person and all that concerned me'.

The distinguished Athenian general Timotheus was the son of Conon, another illustrious commander, and a courtesan. In reply to some banter about his illegitimate birth he once retorted: 'I'm very grateful to my mother for having made me the son of Conon.'

According to Plutarch classical Greece was also familiar with women of loose morals who acted as spies or enemy agents in time of war. He mentions the Ionian Thargelia, whose example was followed, the gossips said, by Aspasia of Miletus. (*Life of Pericles*, 24.) 'Thargelia, both dazzlingly beautiful and extremely shrewd, was the mistress of many of the Greeks. She persuaded all who were attracted by her to join the Great King. In this way, by influencing some of the most powerful personalities in Greece, she sowed the seeds of sympathy for Persia among the citizens.' G. Glotz (*Histoire grec*, t. II, p. 578) writes: 'Thargelia, a cunning and unscrupulous woman, was the chief agent of Persian espionage in Greece. She made many highly placed converts to her cause.'

The ordinary 'peripatetic' prostitutes who solicteid passers-by in the streets and 'took them home' paid a special tax. So did those who were kept in brothels. But the tax was remitted in the case of any woman who went to live with a citizen in his house as a concubine. It appears that Sinope and Phanostrate, named in the speech *Against Androtion* (56) by Demosthenes, came into this category.

In a most ribald scene of the *Ecclesiazusae* by Aristophanes three courtesans, one young and two old, emerge from their dwellings to quarrel in the street over a passing youth. In the *Erotikos* of Plutarch 'a Lais or Gnathenion' kindles her lamp, as evening falls, and 'summons passers-by to enter her house'.

Courtesans of a superior class were employed as entertainers, dancing or playing musical instruments. At least one female oboe player would be present at any private party. In Plato's *Symposium* Eryximachus exclaims: 'Send away that oboe player who has just come in. Let her go and play to herself or, if she likes, to the women in the house.' Such behaviour, however, was an exception, due to the intention to begin a serious philosophical discussion. Towards the end of the proceedings, when Alcibiades enters the apartment,

Greek Hetare Playing for Her Master. Fifth-century red-figured vase-painting. *Bettmann Archive.*

he brings the oboe player back with him and she supports him as he staggers in his intoxication.

Many vase-paintings of banquets show the guests being entertained by oboe players. The latter, after their performance, would go and lie beside anyone who invited them to drink, taking their places on the couches then used at table. These courtesans also took part in the *cottabos* game, when competitors aimed the dregs of their wine at a certain point, pronouncing at the same time the name of a beloved person. A vase-painting by Euphronius depicts a nude woman lying on a dining-couch and holding in her right hand the handle of a libation cup, while she announces: 'I throw for you, Leagrus!' Parlour-games, that of 'Portraits' for instance, were also played at banquets. Forfeits were exacted. One such test consisted in carrying an oboe player round the room a certain number of times.

In the fourth century female musicians, who also played the lyre, harp and tambourine, while others sang, were so much in demand that their fees went up. Aristotle, in his *Constitution of Athens* (50, 2), states that an official body with duties resembling those of modern police superintendents was accordingly appointed to see that such women were not hired at the rate of more than two drachmae an evening, the maximum provided by law, being a sum roughly equivalent to that which a good artisan could earn in a day. Should several clients compete for the same oboe player, lots were drawn under the supervision of this body to decide who should have her.

Women musicians and dancers also performed in groups directed by a 'manager', whose slaves they were. In Xenophon's *Symposium*, for instance, a more realistic rendering of the usual atmosphere of such gatherings than that of Plato, a Syracusan entertainer presents a show comprising several items. His company consists of three young people, a good female oboe player, a female acrobatic dancer and an extremely handsome youth, who both played the lyre and danced. In the final item, a kind of ballet, the dancers played the parts of Dionysus and Ariadne to music by the oboist. The movements were of such a lascivious character that 'the bachelor guests swore they would marry at the first opportunity, while the husbands present left the party on horseback at full gallop, intent on a joyous reunion with their wives'. Respectable women thus occasionally profited from the ardours aroused by the beauty and grace of courtesans! But it must very often have happened that such revels, at which the 'king of the feast' forced his guests to imbibe heavily, ended in orgies. A number of vase-paintings leave us in no doubt that this was the case.

Courtesans also frequented the bathing establishments, which sometimes catered for both sexes and were popular resorts for idlers.

Most *hetairai* were slaves or came from the poorest class. If as children they showed signs of being pretty or, better still, developing good figures—for as we saw in the case of Phryne the Greeks attributed more importance to this feature than to the face—some benevolent female, often their own mothers, would be on hand to undertake their training for the lucrative career they would shortly be in a position to exercise and eventually introduce them to it.

One such procuress is known to us through a speech, *Against Neaera*, erroneously attributed to Demosthenes but actually by another fourth-century Athenian orator. A freedwoman named Nicarete, the wife of a cook, 'showed great skill in discerning the evidence of future beauty in female children. She also understood how to prepare them, in accordance with strict rules, for their future activities. She earned her living that way. The girls passed as her daughters. For those who wished to enjoy their favours would pay more to have the company of free citizens. After she had made a good profit out of each one of them in their earlier years she put them all on sale together, to the number of seven. Their names were Anthea, Stratola, Aristocleia, Metaneira, Philas, Isthmias and Neaera.'

(Top), Dancing Girl and Flute-Player. Red-figured vase-painting. Berlin Museum. *Bettmann Archive.*

(Bottom), Woman Taking Leave of Youth. Red-figured vase-painting by Polygnotus II. Villa Giulia, Rome. *Der Lewismaler*, Henry Roy Williams, Heinrich Keller, Leipzig.

Reading on through this highly instructive speech we learn that the orator Lysias fell in love with one of these seven courtesans, Metaneira, and initiated her into the Eleusinian mysteries.

The youngest, Neaera, eventually came to practice her trade at Corinth, where she acquired a great reputation for beauty. Two of her lovers, after agreeing to share her favours, bought her up for the sum of thirty minae. When they both decided to marry, they paid her off generously. She was thus enabled to purchase her liberty, with the aid of the Athenian Phrynion, whose mistress she also became. But after quarrelling with him she fled to Megara with her three children, two boys and a girl named Phano, and two female attendants. At Megara she met another Athenian, Stephanus, a widower, who took her to live with him, as his wife, at Athens. He even recognised her children, a step which gave rise to the suit against her. Furthermore, he arranged the marriage of Phano to an Athenian who later exercised the office of king-archon. The consequence was that Phano herself became 'queen' for a year, participating as such in the most sacred rites attaching to this function.

Neaera was certainly not the only courtesan who rose from the lowest social level to the middle class by leading a 'gay' life, and finally provided for her children's future through having them recognised by a citizen who grew fond of her. The orator Isaeus, in his speech *On the Estate of Philoctemon* (19–21), tells the following story.

'A certain freedwoman kept a number of girls in a disorderly house which she ran for her own profit at the port of Piraeus.' In this seaport, as at Corinth, such houses were especially numerous, as they always are in ports of any size. 'One of the girls, named Alce, lived for many years in the establishment, until she grew too old for the trade and retired. . . . The aged Euctemon then installed her as the manageress of his property in the Potters' Quarter, near the back street of the wine-sellers. He visited her every rent-day and spent the best part of his time with her, often actually sitting down to meals with the creature, while he left his wife and children and his home to get on without him.'

Finally Euctemon was persuaded by Alce to recognise the eldest of her two sons as his own, in order that the boy might automatically acquire Athenian citizenship on his majority. The suit in which Isaeus appeared arose out of this process of legitimation.

The trade of courtesan was often passed on from mother to daughter, naturally enough. Lais was Timandra's daughter and in the Alexandrine age Oenanthe was the mother of Agathocleia. The mothers presented by Lucian in his *Dialogues of Courtesans* had themselves no doubt been prostitutes and now in their old age relied on their daughters to keep them by adopting the same profession. The whole of the Sixth Dialogue might well be quoted here. It concerns the advice of a poverty-stricken woman to her daughter Corinna, who has just lost her virginity. The mother tells her how a certain successful courtesan made good.

'She began by wearing pretty dresses that were exactly right for her and always being nice to everyone. Without ever bursting into shrieks of laughter like you do, she smiled continually, in the most amiable and inviting fashion. She knew very well how to behave, in every respect, where men were concerned. . . .'

If we can believe what Athenaeus writes in the thirteenth Book of the *Deipnosophistai*, which we have often quoted already, for it is a perfect mine of information about women of loose morals, courtesans received a much more elaborate education, even in the intellectual field, than freeborn Athenian girls. He alleges that the *hetairai* 'applied themselves to study and knowledge of the sciences'. He records a number of witty sayings by one of them, named Glycera.

When, for instance, Stilpo, a philosopher of the Megarian

School, reproached her with corrupting the morals of young men, she is supposed to have retorted:

'You're open to the same charge yourself. For people say that you lead your pupils astray by teaching them useless sophistries, specious arguments. Your "eristics" are as bad as my "erotics". Which is the more dangerous waste of time, to listen to a philosopher or to a courtesan? As Agathon puts it:

> "The frame of a girl may be feeble and weak,
>   but she may have a vigorous mind."'

It was for 'corrupting youth', among other counts in the indictment, that Socrates was condemned to drink hemlock.

As we shall see, several courtesans attended the lectures of Epicurus in his 'Garden'.

Nevertheless, such exceptions to the general rule do not permit the conclusion that the *hetaira* was normally better educated than the freeborn woman. The former, of course, may have known more about the arts of dress and flirtation, as well as music and dancing. For these, together with instruction in deportment, were clearly the chief subjects taught by procuress or mother to the young aspirant to harlotry.

Phryne was physically attractive. But we are not told that she was intelligent, cultivated and witty, like Aspasia. It is possible that the belated renown of courtesans for intellectual refinement arose in part from a calumny and a confusion of ideas. For the Athenian comic poets never tired of repeating that Aspasia led a life of debauchery, though apparently she was as well behaved as she was well informed, and even a scholar.

Both courtesans and their 'trainers' were well aware of the golden rule that governed their profession. Amphis, a poet of the Middle Comedy, expressed it as follows:

'The *hetaira* should always be more obliging than a wife,

makeup

for the very good reason that however disagreeable a wife may be the law compels the husband to keep her. The courtesan, however, knows that she can only retain a lover by lavishing attentions on him. For otherwise he will get another mistress.'

In ancient Greece, just as all over the world today, courtesans made use of rouge, perfume, style in dress, jewellery and every seductive artifice. Respectable women, as indicated in Xenophon's *Oeconomics* (10, 2), also resorted to white lead and henna. But the *hetairai* undoubtedly made up their faces more elaborately and more often.

Eubulus, another poet of the Middle Comedy, thus describes, in his *Garland Sellers*, women whose artificial colours ran in hot weather.

'Two inky streams flow from your eyes. Drops of sweat, falling on your neck, leave trails of rouge. The piles of hair on your forehead are whitened by powder and look like an old woman's.'

The following account of the art of the procuress is given by Alexis, still another writer of comedies.

'They take inexperienced girls to live with them and soon transform not only their characters but also their faces and figures. If they are short, thick cork soles are fixed to their shoes. . . .' High heels were unknown in ancient Greece. But similar effects were produced by the padding of footwear. 'If the hips are insufficiently developed, they are fitted with a quilt which causes people to exclaim: "There's a well-turned rump for you!" If the waist is too thick, it is pinched in with corset-stiffeners. If eyebrows are red, they are blackened with soot. On the other hand, if a girl happens to have any specially attractive physical feature, steps are taken to display it as conspicuously as possible.'

In another passage he refers to 'those fillies of Cypris, expertly broken in, who stand in a row, side by side, in such scanty and transparent garments that they look almost naked. . . . You can buy pleasure, at a price, in such places.'

Just as pederasts (see Chapter 3) proclaimed, by writing on walls, that they admired certain youths, similar inscriptions were also to be found in districts where the *hetairai* lived. Lucian, in the fourth of his *Dialogues of Courtesans*, quotes the statement, written up in the Potters' Quarter: 'Hermotimus the shipowner loves Melitta.' Sometimes these declarations were followed by a note of the sum the lover was prepared to pay.

Courtesans and their admirers exchanged apples as tokens of affection. Aristophanes in the *Clouds* (996–7) advises young men not to frequent the houses of female dancers, 'where, while they are gaping at some little strumpet, she might throw an apple at them'. In the twelfth of Lucian's *Dialogues of Courtesans* a jealous *hetaira* complains to her lover:

'You took a bite from an apple and leant forward to flip it cleverly into Pyrallis's bosom, without even trying to stop me seeing you. And then she kissed the apple and slipped it into her bust-bodice, between her breasts.'

As we shall see in Chapter 7, the apple also played an important part in the love-story of Acontius and Cydippe.

Athenaeus reports (567 c–d) that Eubulus called one of his comedies *Clepsydra*. This was the nickname of a courtesan who had such a constant flow of patrons that she only allowed each of them the exact time taken by her water-clock (*klepsudra*) to run out. We should say that she regulated supplies of love, like gas or electricity, 'by meter'.

As already noted in the previous chapter, the Hellenistic age was characterised by many economic, social and religious changes in Greek life. National habits, accordingly, also altered. A. Aymard (op. cit.) records that 'Alexander's campaign has been compared by historians with the discovery of America, which inaugurated modern times'. The import of Persian gold and the opening up of wide regions of Asia and Africa to Greek industry and commerce, brought about rapid increases in comfort and luxury. At the same time ideals were transformed. The word *truphe*, for

example, had in the classical period a mainly pejorative
sense, meaning a soft and easy, sensual and undisciplined
mode of life. But in the third century it began to imply a
compliment, as designating the most refined type of civilisation.

Courtesans, naturally, were among the first to profit from
these changes. The taste for pleasure, luxury and dissipation
descended to new social levels, as poverty was replaced by
affluence or even great wealth. Moreover, since pederasty
was by then, we may suppose, in decline, the ladies in
question must have had so many rich clients that they
scarcely knew, so to speak, which way to turn.

The real capital of this new, cosmopolitan world was
Alexandria. Its civilisation is known as either the Hellenistic
or the Alexandrine. At one time many schoolboys were fond
of surreptitiously reading Pierre Louys's novel *Aphrodite*,
which purports to describe the lives of certain *hetairai* at
Alexandria. The book is too artificial and exaggerated to
pass as a realistic picture of its subject. But the general
impression it leaves is not altogether misleading.

Many courtesans already figure in the New Comedy,
though hardly any are to be found in the plays of Aristophanes. Most of these women are represented as heartless,
greedy, mendacious and profligate. But sometimes they are
themselves caught in their own traps and fall genuinely in
love, as Lais did with Hippolochus. They then become the
devoted and faithful companions of a single lover. Even those
who are not 'reborn' in this way occasionally arouse a
reader's sympathy. Habrotonon, for instance, in Menander's
Arbitration, (see Chapter 4) amiably agrees to console
Charisius during his temporary estrangement from his wife
Pamphyle and eventually, with disinterested benevolence,
reconciles the young couple by clearing up the misunder-
standing which had caused their separation.

Both the New Comedy and the lyrical verse of the
Alexandrine age were imitated by the Roman poets. Each

type of production often refers to the practice of lovers, when disdained by top-ranking courtesans, of serenading the lady in question. They were in the habit of spending the night on her doorstep, uttering vain entreaties and special 'dirges of the closed door'. This custom is mentioned in one of the *Love Letters* composed by Aristaenetus. A very practically minded courtesan writes to an aspirant:

'No *hetaira* is ever excited by an oboe or captivated by a lyre unless hard cash is brought into the picture. Our only idol is money. We can't be caught by melodies. . . .'

Aristaenetus lived in the fifth century A.D. But he was regularly inspired by previous authors, especially those of the Alexandrine age.

Alexander himself, and particularly his successors, known as the Diadochi, loved to be surrounded by a positive harem of fair and frail ladies. Some of them became great favourites or even married their patrons. As Plutarch writes in his *Erotikos* (753 D–F):

'Female oboe players and Samian dancers, like Aristonica or Oenanthe with her tambourine or Agathocleia, trampled the diadems of kings underfoot.'

Agathocleia, the daughter of Oenanthe, became the mistress of Ptolemy IV Philopator, Pharaoh of Egypt. According to the staid historian Polybius she 'dominated his mind and convulsed the entire kingdom'.

Plutarch continues: 'And was not Belestiche, as Zeus is my witness, originally a barbarian slave bought in the public market? Yet she now owns, at Alexandria, shrines and temples which the besotted king'—he was Ptolemy II Philadelphus—'has consecrated to her in dedicating them to Aphrodite-Belestiche!'

Plutarch also wrote a life of Demetrius Poliorcetes—the surname means 'taker of cities'—in which the character of that famous soldier is delineated. For the author this time intended, instead of producing edifying biographies, to confront his readers with an example to be avoided, just as the Spartans used to show their children a drunken helot in order to warn them against the perils of strong liquors.

'Demetrius', he declares, 'was a much-married man. He lived with several wives, not to mention the concubines and courtesans he gathered about him, to such an extent that his sensuality made him the most disreputable king of his time. ... His booty in Cyprus included the celebrated Lamia, who had originally been prized for her musical talent, since she was a tolerable oboe player. Later on she became renowned for her loose morals. When Demetrius met her she was already past her best and much older than he was. Yet she contrived to obtain such a hold over him that she may be considered the only woman he ever really loved. In other cases he simply let himself be loved. ... At Athens he lived on the Acropolis. But, far from respecting the virgin goddess Athena, he committed so many shameful outrages upon the persons of freeborn Athenian children and women that the sanctity of that holy place was less profaned by the hours he spent there with Chrysis, Lamia, Demo and Anticyra, all notorious harlots.'

The extreme indulgence shown in the Hellenistic period, with its worship of *truphe*, to the most dissolute behaviour, can hardly be wondered at. For the two chief philosophical doctrines of that epoch, almost equivalent to religions in the minds of the most cultivated Greeks of the day, openly advocated debauch. The Stoics of the Portico recommended homosexuality, while the Epicureans of the Garden argued that heterosexual love should be reduced to purely physical experience, in order to eliminate the annoyance and anxiety which the sentiment as such was bound eventually to produce.

Only two women ever attended Plato's Academy lectures. Epicurus had as many as seven, quite a group. The figures are a definite indication of feminine progress in the intellectual field. Yet on a closer view we find that six of Epicurus's pupils were well-known courtesans. They were Leontion, the

master's favourite, Mammarion, Hedeia, whose name means
'the sweet one', Erotion (derived from Eros), Nicidion and
Demelata. Father Festugière gravely comments in his
excellent little book entitled *Epicurus and his Gods:*

'This large number of *hetairai* appears rather astonishing
at first and no doubt their presence at the school gave rise to
disturbing rumours.'

Well, that incorrigible gossip Athenaeus does remark in
this connection:

'Was not Leontion, that most notorious courtesan, the
mistress of Epicurus? Nor did her character change after she
began to study philosophy. For in the shady nooks of the
Garden she submitted to the embraces of all his disciples and
made no secret of her affair with the Master himself. He was
very attentive to her, too, as is evident from his *Letters to
Hermarchus.*'

It would 'appear rather astonishing', I think, to anyone
who understands the Epicurean theory of pleasure, if those
'disturbing rumours' had no foundation in fact!

Earlier in this chapter we noted that Socrates mentioned
erotic witchcraft in his conversation with the courtesan
Theodote. This source and the verses of Pindar to be quoted
shortly prove that, though such rites were especially widespread in the Hellenistic and Roman periods, they were by
no means unknown in fifth-century Greece.

We may briefly refer to these practices here. They were
not, however, performed exclusively by courtesans. Married
women, too, occasionally indulged in them. Nor were certain
auxiliary implements, which highly sexed ladies temporarily
deprived of masculine partners employed, only put into
operation by *hetairai*. The 'two friends' in the Sixth Mime of
Herondas are perfectly respectable housewives. Nevertheless,
we have reason to believe that erotic witchcraft, like the
excessive use of cosmetics, was mainly in vogue among
courtesans, at any rate during the Alexandrine era.

Simaetha, in the Idyll of Theocritus entitled *The Witches*,
may or may not have been a *hetaira*. She certainly seems to be

living alone with one slave, which would be surprising if she were a respectable girl. Neither her father, mother nor family are mentioned.

In any case she has been deserted by Delphis, a young man to whom she had given herself. Her one idea now is to get him back by any means in her power or, if that proves impossible, to cause his death. The process of casting spells for this purpose can be deduced from the many tablets of anathema which have survived. Some of these date back to the fourth century. Simaetha sings:

'As I melt this wax by the aid of the goddess, so may Myndian Delphis this instant melt with love. And as this brazen disc turns distraught under Aphrodite's hand, so distraught may he turn upon my threshold.'

The following line serves as a refrain all through the first section of the Idyll:

'*Iynx*, lure to my dwelling this man, my lover!'

The brazen disc is the wheel to which the magic bird called *iynx* was attached. The rite is already known to us through Pindar, who attributes its invention to Aphrodite herself. The context is that of the love which Jason must inspire in Medea, the princess of Colchis, in order to win the Golden Fleece. (Pyth. IV, 213–15.)

'The goddess of Cyprus, on Mount Olympus, fastened to an unbreakable wheel the *iynx* of variegated plumage, binding it by all four extremities. Thus she sent for the first time upon mankind the bird of frenzy. . . .'

The *iynx* is the wryneck, so called on account of its ability to move its head in any direction. It is therefore obviously associated with the wheel, so that the word *iynx* came to connote the combination of both. The wheel could have the significance of a 'magic circle'. A fifth-century vase-painting represents the mother of an Athenian girl, on the morning of her daughter's marriage, making the magic wheel spin round a wand, so as to attract the gifts of Aphrodite to the young couple. Such 'birds with wheels', mostly in terracotta, have been identified in many museums. They must originally have been used in witchcraft of this kind.

Lucian's *Dialogues of Courtesans* (1 and 4) make several allusions to erotic magic.

'Do you actually suppose, Thais, that Gorgona attracted that lover of mine simply by her beauty? Don't you know that Chrysarion, her mother, is a witch who has learnt Thessalian incantations and can bring the moon down upon the earth? It's even said that she flies about in the air during the night. It was she who drove the fellow crazy by giving him her potions and now the two of them are fleecing him.'

Another *hetaira* named Melitta asks her friend Bacchis to recommend a witch who can restore her lover's affection:

'BACCHIS. I know one who's very clever, my dear. She's Syrian by birth and still quite hale and hearty. She got me back Phanias, who'd quarrelled with me for no good reason, just like your Charinus.

MELITTA. How did she do it? Can you remember?

BACCHIS. She's not expensive, Melitta. She only asks one drachma and a loaf. But you'll also have to take her some salt, seven obols and a torch. She'll need, too, a bowl of watered wine, all of which she drinks herself. Then she must have something belonging to the man, clothes, shoes, hair or anything like that.

MELITTA. I've got a pair of his shoes.

BACCHIS. Well, she'll hang them on a nail and burn sulphur under them, scattering salt on the flames. Then she speaks your two names, yours and your lover's. After that she takes a wheel from her bosom and spins it, babbling a magic formula very fast. It has dreadful words in it that make you shudder. That's what she did in my case. Soon afterwards Phanias came back to me, in spite of the remonstrances of his friends and the urgent entreaties of Phoebis, with whom he was living. It was the incantation which did most to bring him back. At the same time she taught me a secret way to make him conceive a violent hatred of Phoebis. It was to keep a look-out for her footprints and if I could find one to put my right foot into the mark made by her left and my left into the one made by her right. I was to say at the same time: 'I'm trampling on you, I'm above you.' So I did what she told me.

MELITTA. Don't let's waste another moment, Bacchis. Send for that Syrian right away. And, Acis—[*she turns to her maid*]—get that loaf ready, and the sulphur and all the rest of it, for the incantation.'

The permanent popularity of courtesans in ancient Greece is surely the best proof that homosexuals were either not consistently so or not particularly numerous. We have already suggested that inversion was never very prevalent except in one class of society and over quite a limited period.

In 346 B.C. Demosthenes and Aeschines were members of an Athenian embassy sent to Philip of Macedon. Aeschines reported later (*On the Disloyal Embassy*, 112) that Demosthenes had allowed himself a certain amount of jesting in his speech to the king. 'He repeatedly excused himself by such remarks as the following: "I haven't said that you are good-looking, for the best-looking human beings are women. Nor have I said that you are a champion drinker. For that would be to compare you with a sponge. . . ."'

The sally of Demosthenes at this date about women being the best looking of human beings is significant enough. (See Chapter 4 for social changes in the fourth century.) But I would myself regard it as valid for all Greek history. For even in Homer's works a kind of halo is cast by feminine beauty on the passages of the *Iliad* and *Odyssey* where Helen appears.

We may assume, in fact, that the great majority of the ancient Greeks, at practically all periods, considered, like Demosthenes, that 'the best-looking human beings are women'.

6

PHILOSOPHERS OF LOVE

'Marriage is a source of friendship. For it is a common participation in great mysteries.'

PLUTARCH.

THE ancient Greeks invented science, history and philosophy. Nothing under the sun escaped their curiosity, their attention and their reflection. It was natural, therefore, that they should take up the study of normal attraction between the sexes, of friendship and of the homosexuality which, as we found in Chapter 3, was so often illustrated among them.

The question of their vocabulary in this connection has first to be considered. 'Love' is used by modern Europeans in a great many senses. One 'loves' certain sorts of food, one's brother, one's wife, one's children or God. The ancient Greek word *philia* has equally various and definite meanings, but differing in certain respects from those of our 'love'. It is usually translated 'friendship' but really has a wider significance, including every kind of attachment and affection between two persons. Four such types of sentiment were distinguished by philosophers. There was the *philia* felt for one another by blood-relations, the *philia* extended to guests, arising from the importance attributed to hospitality in the antique world, the *philia* which was exactly what we ourselves mean by 'friendship', and finally the passionate *philia* which may exist between persons either of the same or of different sexes.

One consequence of these distinctions was that the famous Pythagorean maxim, 'Between friends all is held in common', normally included all the four categories mentioned above and not simply 'friendship' in the narrow modern sense.

There were also many other words in Greek denoting a number of related varieties of affection not covered by *philia* and *eros*. Thus *eunoia* meant benevolence and devotion, *agape* disinterested love, *storge* tenderness, *pothos* physical desire, *charis* gratitude and generosity, and *mania* frenzied passion. Nor is this list at all exhaustive.

The word *agape* is not often found in pagan texts. But it was destined for an important future, since the early Christians and the Greek Fathers of the Church used it to mean both the love of God and the fraternal affection characteristic of their gatherings, which they actually called *agapai*. They did not care for the word *eros*, naturally.

As stated in Chapter 2, Aphrodite and especially Eros, in so far as they stood for the 'universal mutual attraction' between animate beings, were considered by poets like Hesiod to be primitive divinities who had presided over the organisation of the cosmos. From this standpoint Orphic theogony forms a bridge between the antique poets and the first philosophers.

Heraclitus of Ephesus lived through the end of the sixth century B.C. and the beginning of the fifth. Empedocles of Agrigentum flourished in the middle of the fifth century. Both philosophers regarded love and its opposite, hate, as physical forces affecting the entire universe. In the view of Heraclitus harmony arose through the union of contraries. 'That which is opposed is useful,' he said, 'and it is from struggle that the best harmony is born. All is created by discord.' He believed, therefore, that conflict or war, the *eris* of Hesiod, preceded Eros. But he added that 'the discordant accords with itself, the reconciliation being effected by inverse tensions, as in the arch or the lyre'. Evolution is a compromise between contraries, producing harmony, which is thus not a beginning but an end.

Empedocles, on the other hand, started with the four

material elements or constituent principles of the universe, water, earth, fire and air. Their organisation was due to two cosmic forces, Love and Hate. The poet—for Empedocles wrote in verse—designates Love by the words *philotes* (equivalent to *philia*), *storge* or *harmonia*, or else by the names Aphrodite and Cypris. He maintained, in direct opposition to Heraclitus, that like attracts like.

But we need not stay to examine such speculations, for they assumed love to be a 'physical' principle of the universe, not a human sentiment. We may pass on immediately to Socrates, who 'brought philosophy down from heaven to earth' by making the primary object of thought knowledge of mankind.

In Chapters 3 and 5 the subjects of pederastic education and the visit of Socrates to the courtesan Theodote led us to allude to his ideas about love. Here we may define them a little more closely, avoiding as far as possible the introduction of the views of his disciple Plato. Socrates himself wrote nothing. So we can only discover what he thought by reading the works of his pupils, Plato and Xenophon in particular.

Socrates often declared that he knew only one science, that of love. As he was fond of striking and even disconcerting metaphors, he proclaimed himself to be a pander or procurer (see Xenophon, *Symposium*, IV, 62) comparable with either the women who earned their living by training future courtesans and launching them at the right moment or with the men who supplied pederasts with their beloved youths.

But naturally all his listeners knew perfectly well that such expressions were only a sprinkling of 'attic salt' over his meaning. Just as he said that he was a midwife, like his mother, because he tried to 'bring to birth' the minds of his disciples, so his function as pander or procurer was exercised solely in an intellectual or spiritual sense. His deepest love was for philosophy (see Plato, *Gorgias*, 482 a), hence for the education of young men, whom he longed to guide towards the goals of truth and virtue.

He has been called in modern times a mystic with a sensual imagination. However that may be, it is certain that he considered chastity an essential condition of freedom of mind. He had no objection to love in itself. But he condemned its development into carnal passion for the reason that it then disturbed the intelligence and by its violence drove out liberty and logic. He compared Euthydemus in the act of approaching his lover Critias with a pig rubbing itself against a stone. (See Xenophon, *Memorabilia*, I, 2, 30.)

He maintained that there were two loves, personified by the earthly (*pandemos*) and the heavenly (*urania*) Aphrodite. Mere satisfaction of the sexual instinct mistook the true aim of love, which was the well-being, i.e. the moral perfection, of the beloved person. The purely physical type of pederast debased and degraded the object of his desire. His love was a vice. To attribute such conduct to gods and heroes was to insult them.

Pure love, on the other hand, was indispensable to all progress towards virtue. This kind of love inspired teachers and induced pupils to follow them along the right road.

If therefore, we confine ourselves strictly to the works of Xenophon, not an original thinker and thus far less inclined than Plato to introduce his own ideas among those of his master, we shall find that Socrates, for all the boldness of his metaphors and language, was a stern moralist. There was no question, in his view, of purifying physical passion, which could never be anything but low and vulgar, but of eradicating it completely and replacing it by exclusively psychological affection. The famous 'theory of ideas' had yet to be born. Plato, the disciple of Socrates, was to invent and develop it, with a brilliance known to all the world.

It is not without interest to remember in the first place that Socrates was married—though unhappily, his wife Xanthippe being a shrew—and that he condemned physical homosexuality. Plato, however, remained a bachelor all his

life and had a great many 'special friends'. In questions of
love, accordingly, that philosopher's personal experience is
likely to have had some influence upon his thought.

It is true that Plato never expressly preached any love but
that of the mind, which we still call today 'platonic love'.
But, though he nowhere compares himself with a pander or
procurer, he makes a great many references to pederasty in
a much more indulgent tone than his master's and sometimes
even with enthusiasm. It was not until he came to write his
last work, the *Laws*, which he did not live to finish, that he
committed himself to unmistakable condemnation of homosexuality.

In his view all love had a natural tendency to involve
generosity and magnanimity. It only became subject to
shameful disorder by accident. He continued to uphold the
distinction made by Socrates between the two Aphrodites,
earthly and heavenly. But the transition between the two,
in his opinion, was easy. He could see the promise of pure
affection even in the most disgraceful of sexual intimacies.
He considered that in guilty unions their normal development had been arrested before they could arrive at the
'sublimation' implicit in their nature.

On the other hand it is clear that conjugal affection
hardly deserved, in his judgment, the glorious name of *eros*.
He shared the common outlook of his day in regarding
marriage as a mere convenience for supplying families and
the State with children. For this reason he could easily bring
himself, in the *Republic*, to ordain that women should be held
in common by the warrior class, so as to elimate the jealousy
arising from ownership and even the idea of possession itself.
This odd form of communism caused Plato to do violence to
the very nature of love as a sentiment confined to two persons
only. We have already seen, in Chapter 4, that certain
Spartan customs based on eugenics may have led the
philosopher astray in this direction.

With the above reservations, in my opinion serious, it may

be affirmed that no other ancient Greek has praised love so warmly, both as philosopher and as artist in words.

The *Lysis* provides no more than a slight introduction to the investigation of erotic *philia*. Moreover, it ends abruptly with a confession of at least temporary failure. Nevertheless, it is a good example of what A. Dies (*Autour de Platon*, p. 418) calls 'the courts of love constituted by the schools and gymnasia of Plato's time'. For this reason the dialogue in question was quoted in Chapter 3. But it is only in the *Symposium* and the *Phaedo* that the Platonic theory of love is clearly expounded.

The first five speeches in the *Symposium* are made by Phaedo, Pausanias, Eryximachus, Aristophanes and Agathon. But they are only partial and misleading approaches to the views later advanced by Socrates. We need do no more than pause for a moment to note the extraordinary remarks of Aristophanes the dramatist, upon whom Plato fathers a fanciful kind of anthropology.

Humanity began, he says, with three sexes, not two, as at present. These earliest of mankind were monsters 'with spherical backs and sides, each having four hands, four legs, two faces and four ears ... their private parts being also duplicated'. The first sex had two male organs and the second two female organs, while the third was an *androgyne*, both male and female. The masculine beings were offshoots of the sun, the feminine of the earth, and the androgyne of the moon. 'For the moon shares the natures of the two other astral bodies.'

These creatures were the Giants, who planned to storm heaven. Zeus and the other gods, in order to render their strength and insolence harmless, decided to weaken their dual bodies by halving them. The Giants were accordingly, so to speak, sawn in two, 'as one cuts an egg with a hair'. Then Apollo turned their faces and necks to the cut side. He also undertook more detailed operations, which we should call plastic surgery.

This weird myth concludes as follows.

'We are all therefore complementary fractions of humanity, tokens of our species, and, owing to the cut, are like plaice, the duplication of a single form. So we are all constantly looking for our complementary fraction, the token, of ourselves. Thus men who are the halves of the composite androgyne being are all fond of women. Most adultererers are of this sort, which also provides women who are fond of men and commit adultery.'

We may stop here to observe that the myth is certainly an excellent illustration of the expression 'better half', of which an early variant is Corneille's line: 'Render thyself worth the name of my chaste half.' But, concerned as Plato is in this case with ardent, irresistible passion, it never occurs to him to mention husband and wife, but only adulterers. As a bachelor and champion of uranian love he cannot imagine deep affection between man and woman except outside marriage or in violation of its contract. Yet Phaedo's speech (179 a–e) had praised the conjugal devotion of Alcestis. All the same, he thought a good deal more of the devotion of Achilles to his lover Patroclus.

Aristophanes, in other words Plato, continues:

'Women cut from the second, feminine sex don't pay the least attention to us men. On the contrary, it's women they are inclined to. That's the species to which the darlings of some ladies we know belong! Then there are men who are slices cut from the masculine. They pursue males. Such a person, while he is a youth, since he's a miniature cut from an original male, is fond of adult males and likes to sleep with and embrace them. Boys and adolescents so given are always the most noticeable, for their nature is in the highest degree virile. It's true that some people call them shameless. But that's wrong. They don't behave like that because they're shameless, but because they have determined characters, the heart of a man and the bearing of a male who is eager in the pursuit of those like him.'

We may remark in passing that the theory of Empedocles, who maintained that like attracts like, could plausibly be applied to explain homosexuality, while that of Heraclitus, the attraction of opposites, would suit heterosexual love better.

The rest of this passage from the *Symposium* need not be quoted, for in Plato the subject of homosexuality is treated at inordinate length.

The myth attributed to Aristophanes takes an extremely favourable view, as we have seen, of all the varieties of love. Socrates then relates a second myth, which he says he heard from a priestess, Diotima of Mantinea, a most learned lady. She alleged that Love was not a god but a 'demon', in other words a being half divine and half human, corresponding to some extent with the Christian 'angel', originally conceived as a 'messenger'.

It appears that the gods once held a feast to celebrate the birth of Aphrodite. At this banquet—for the belief that Eros was the son of Aphrodite had to be accounted for somehow—Poverty became pregnant by Expediency, who was drunk on nectar. Love, therefore, is poor and destitute, like his mother. He is 'rough and squalid, a vagabond with nowhere to lay his head, always sleeping out of doors on the hard ground or spending the night on doorsteps or the open road.' So he is also a tough male and, like his father, 'on the watch for everything beautiful and good, a first-rate hunter, deeply interested in inventions and highly resourceful. He is an incomparable sorcerer, sophist and philosopher.' But his intermediate nature keeps him half-way between ignorance and knowledge, like philosophers who 'love wisdom' and always pursue it in vain. He, too, incessantly gives chase to the Beautiful and Good, never possesses them but is obsessed by an ineradicable and ardent desire to do so.

Diotima tells Socrates (205 d–e):

'I know there is a theory that lovers are in quest of their own halves. But in my opinion the object of love is neither a half nor a whole.'

This scornful reference certainly seems aimed at the ideas expressed in the speech by Aristophanes. For Diotima and consequently for Socrates or rather Plato love tends to 'cause birth in beauty, both physically and mentally. . . . Sexual union results in birth, a phenomenon in which there is something divine. Fecundity and procreation even bestow an immortal character upon the mortal agent of them.'

But this desire for a perpetual projection of the self can be satisfied on a much higher level, that of spiritual fertility. In this case the most 'philosophical' type of love, the homosexual, is alone concerned. The great poets, inventors and lawgivers were all inspired by it. It was the love of the Beautiful which impelled them to acquire immortality by noble deeds.

Complete initiation begins with the love of a single admirable body, continues with the realisation that the beauty of an individual is paralleled by that of other individuals and goes on to esteem the beauty of the soul more highly than that of the body, thus rising by successive stages to ultimate knowledge, the culmination of which is the revelation of immaterial, divine and eternal beauty, in a word, God.

Such are the steps of the argument by which love among handsome youths and their admirers is made the first rung upon a spiritual ladder which all philosophers are called upon to ascend. Thus love, which is sometimes said to blind its devotees, is made by Plato the indispensable condition of the highest flights of intelligence and supreme mental illumination.

In the *Phaedo* Socrates distinguishes four kinds of ecstasy (*mania*), otherwise divine possession (*enthousiasmos*), conferred upon mankind for its good by heaven. They comprise the prophetic ecstasy of the priestess of the Pythian oracle, the religious ecstasy of the Dionysian or Corybantic mysteries, the poetic ecstasy imparted by the Muses, and finally, most elevated of all, the amorous ecstasy conducive to omniscience.

The human soul, which is immortal and remembers

previous existences, resembles a winged pair of horses driven by the charioteer Reason. One of the pair is docile, representing courage, the will of the righteous, and one is restive, typical of the desire for pleasure. In order that the chariot may rise and follow the celestial procession of souls mounting towards the blessed company of the gods, the wings of the horses must be made to grow. Vigorous wings like those of Eros are only attainable by the soul through its contemplation of earthly beauty, which reminds it of the ideal beauty contemplated in a former state of existence. The soul can then obtain access to the loftiest region of all, that of the Ideas or eternal forms, where it will once more contemplate the divine essence.

Thus amorous ecstasy, the fourth category of superhuman inspiration, appears to be the finest and most precious of all, for it makes lovers the superiors of prophets, initiates and poets. Accordingly, it is only through love of handsome youths that one will eventually have the chance of 'that blessed and divine vision' of remote realities which might almost be translated 'beatitude'.

It is clear that this theory of love is by no means purely intellectualist. Emile Bréhier (*Histoire de la Philosophie*, I, 110) writes: 'The theme of Eros and that of divine inspiration in general in Plato's thought reveals its emotional basis.' L. Robin considers, in fact, that for Plato 'Love is both impulsive and educative, composed of the principles of both action and understanding. . . . It is revealed as a means of liberating not only the senses but also the personality. In relation to the body as to the soul it is a kind of symbol of the specific longing for immortality and universality. According to the *Phaedo* it is the most effective way of restoring to the soul the wings it has lost, so that it can escape from earthly existence even before that existence ends.'

In our rapid survey of Greek theories of love we shall now come down to earth, without returning to the intoxicating and rarefied atmosphere of the heights to which we were summoned by Plato's genius. We shall find more ordinary good sense and precise observation in certain of his successors. We may start with Aristotle, who heard his lectures at the Academy, but was an original and profound thinker on his own account. It has been said that while his master showed philosophy the way to the Idea, Aristotle pointed out the road to the Real.

He dealt rather with friendship than with love. The former was for him the most important of human sentiments owing to its attraction to virtue, the essential ingredient of moral character. Beauty, on the contrary, to which love is attracted, was considered by Aristotle an accidental and transitory quality. For love is based on pleasure, the nature of which is altered by time. Love is undoubtedly a stronger and more violent emotion. But friendship is to be preferred as more durable.

In the Nicomachean Ethics (VIII, 3) he writes:

'It is the young who are most prone to love, which is as a rule the result only of desire and aims simply at pleasure. That is why young people fall in and out of love so easily, changing their minds twenty times a day.'

We may pause to reflect that Aristotle's praise of friendship unquestionably bears in mind those relations of mutual esteem, affection and tenderness which may arise between two persons of different sex, for example in marriage, which is, in principle at least, a stable institution.

The leading virtue in Aristotelian ethics is magnanimity. The magnanimous man is in a sense self-sufficient. Yet, since human beings are sociable by nature, he needs friends. In fact, as R.-A. Gauthier writes in this connection, 'friendship is a necessary condition of the practice of virtue. A virtuous friend is indispensable to the virtuous man, who thus obtains the opportunity to do good, since nothing is more enjoyable than to do good to a friend out of sheer affection for him. Friendship also teaches the magnanimous man the pleasures of entertaining company, as well as the glory of self-sacrifice, perhaps the highest manifestation of human capacity, the very summit of grandeur and beauty.' On this view Alcestis, who gave her life for her husband, was surely an outstanding example of magnanimity.

Aristotle had less intellectual ambition than Plato. He did not aim so high. But his conceptions were more exact and realistic. He always kept his feet on the ground and never lost his head in the clouds. Plato disregarded so unexceptionable a sentiment as conjugal affection. Aristotle, as already noted, married twice, to his entire satisfaction, and took the most serious account of such natural ties, which also depend for their strength on *philia*.

He observes in the Nicomachean Ethics (VIII, 12, 7), a work addressed to Nicomachus, his son by his second wife, Herpyllis, as noted in Chapter 5:

'Between husband and wife mutual affection (*philia*) seems to be an effect of nature. For human beings are more naturally inclined to live in couples than in urban society, all the more so since the family is older than the city, as well as more necessary, and also since reproduction is a faculty common to all mankind. But in the case of other animate beings union is not prolonged, whereas man takes a partner not only for the sake of procreation but even more to obtain that which he regards as indispensable to existence. . . . Both parties help each other and share the advantages proper to each. Thus, in this kind of affection the useful is combined with the agreeable. Such unions can even be based on virtue if both partners are honest. . . . It also appears that children constitute a bond between them. For this reason barren associations are the more rapidly dissolved, children being the common property of the parents and everything which the latter hold in common preserving harmony between them. To enquire into the proper conduct of a husband towards his wife and in general the behaviour of friends to each other is obviously the same thing as to enquire how the principles of justice are to be upheld.'

It would be no exaggeration to say that Aristotle was the first to rehabilitate conjugal affection in the eyes of philosophers by including it explicitly in the category of *philia*, which is the path of virtue.

Like Socrates, Aristotle takes a stern view of pederasty. He puts it among the depraved tastes which he describes as 'sometimes instinctive, sometimes the results of habits contracted in childhood'. He hesitates to regard it as a malady or a vice, a form of 'bestiality' or 'intemperance'. But he generally considers it a pathological act and abhors it. He only refers to homosexuality incidentally, as a tendency more prevalent among foreigners than Greeks, which is a good reason for discrediting it. He censures the Cretan lawgiver for having instituted 'reciprocal male intercourse', and adds:

'The Celts and certain other barbarian nations openly favour homosexuality.' (*Politics*, II, 6–7.)

In the same work (IV, 14) he gives some good advice relative to marriage and the best conditions in which to have children. The passage, which deserves quotation in full, contains the following important paragraphs.

'The limits of the procreative faculty being fixed for males at not more than sixty-two and for females at fifty, these ages should be taken into consideration when calculating those at which marriage should be entered upon. Girls ought to marry towards their eighteenth year and men towards their thirty-seventh, or perhaps a little before. . . .'

Here Aristotle seems to realise that his theoretical difference of twenty years between the ages of men and women on marriage may be, in spite of its advantages, a pretty wide one. He goes on:

'The infidelity of either partner should be considered shameful and infamous so long as the ties of marriage exist. If adultery is committed during the procreative period, the punishment should be severe enough to correspond with so grave a breach of decency.'

We have already noted that Greek public opinion viewed the

adultery of a husband very lightly. Aristotle, however, affirms that each party would be equally to blame in such an affair.

Accordingly, Aristotle's attitude to love retains no trace of the previous prejudice of philosophers in favour of pederasty. If he were our only witness on the subject we might even be perfectly justified in declining to think of homosexuality as specifically Greek.

He also uses quite unprecedented language in referring to conjugal affection. We may well suppose that in this connection his outlook reflects the social development indicated in Chapter 4, which took place in his lifetime. Women were by then beginning to emerge from the moral isolation to which they were often condemned in the sixth and fifth centuries. It is easy to understand that since that epoch they had come to be increasingly regarded as companions capable of inspiring affection and confidence as well as carnal desire, sentiments, in short, of true *philia*.

The Garden, in other words the School of Epicurus, stands in far more radical opposition to the Academy than does the Lyceum of Aristotle. In erotics especially, but also in many other respects, Epicurus appears as almost the antithesis of Plato.

Plato considered love to be a gift of the gods, a superhuman inspiration. Epicurus retorts that it is 'not sent by the gods'. It is reduced by him to 'an impetuous appetite for sexual pleasure, accompanied by frenzy and torment'. In short, he deprives *eros* of its independence by identifying it with lust for carnal intercourse, which he denounces as the worst enemy of the serenity of the wise man.

Incidentally, he hardly ever mentions the word *eros*. The only sentiment which he, in common with all the Greek philosophers, extols, is friendship, *philia*. But he is careful not to extend its meaning, as Aristotle did, to cover conjugal affection. Friendship in the restricted sense thus given to *philia* formed at once the cement and the institutional basis of the Epicurean School.

The Epicureans were by no means hostile to women. The School had a number of female members, though all but one happened to be courtesans. The gossip of Athenaeus already referred to about the affair between Epicurus and Leontion may be only slander. But, all the same, it is unlikely that a strict moral tone prevailed in such an atmosphere. As for homosexuality, it does not appear that Epicurus ever encouraged it. His disciple Philodemus even expressly condemns it.

In practice the Epicurean outlook closely resembled that of an egotistical old bachelor, valuing peace of mind above all things, and dignifying it with the high-sounding name of 'philosophic wisdom'. According to Epicurus, 'Sexual intercourse never did anybody any good and one can think oneself lucky if it doesn't do one harm. A wise man will neither marry nor have children. Nor will he yield to the passion of love.' At first sight, therefore, his views seem to involve celibacy and chastity.

But Epicurus had to face the question how those who had fallen victims to amorous desire could recover the serenity of wisdom. For his own classification placed love in the category of natural, if unnecessary, desires. He admitted, accordingly, that in certain circumstances the wise man might marry and have children. But it is clear that the philosopher hoped such marriages would be based on reason rather than genuine affection. For if not, what would become of the wise man's serenity in the hands of a wife?

This attitude is not unlike that of St. Paul (1 Cor. VII, 8–9) when he wrote: 'It is better to marry than to burn.' But marriage is the only 'remedy for concupiscence' permitted by the Apostle, whereas Epicurus writes to a young man tormented by sexual desire: 'Don't hesitate to do as you wish.' In his opinion to satisfy a craving was to recover one's equanimity for the time being, though in the end, as Baudelaire wrote in *Le Voyage*, 'desire grows by what it feeds on'.

Epicurus's own position appears slightly ambiguous. But

Head of Epicurus. Life-size, stone. *The Metropolitan Museum of Art, Rogers Fund, 1911.*

this impression may be due to the fact that we possess only fragments of his works. The views of the Roman poet Lucretius, an impassioned and fanatical epicurean, are much more definite. So far as they concern love I believe them to represent, if not always the master's own thought, at any rate that of most of his followers.

The teaching that emerges from Book IV of the *De Natura Rerum* by Lucretius is distinct and perfectly simple. It makes a clean break between the sentiment of love, which it regards as fraught with disaster, and the physical pleasure of sexual intercourse, which it recommends as beneficent.

The attitude of Lucretius in this matter is to some extent anticipated by that of the hedonist (pleasure-lover) Aristippus of Cyrene, author of the remark about his mistress, the courtesan Lais, already quoted.

'She doesn't love me, you say? That doesn't matter to me. I don't suppose fish or wines love me either. But I take pleasure in both all the same.'

Lucretius declares:

'It is best to reject all that can keep our love in being and turn our minds to other things, to cast into the first body that comes our way the liquor which has accumulated in our own rather than preserve it for a single beloved individual, thus ensuring trouble and grief for ourselves. For if we cherish our love, the abscess swells up again and becomes an inveterate sore. Day by day the frenzy grows and the pain will be harder to bear, if you do not efface its first wounds by new scars, submitting your injuries, while they are still fresh, to the cares of vagrant Venus'—the Roman equivalent of Aphrodite Pandemos—'wherever you may happen to meet her. To avoid the passion of love is not to deprive oneself of the joys of Venus but on the contrary to savour their delights without undergoing their exactions.'

The last phrase might serve as a motto for the debauched libertines of all ages. It suggests the same difference between Venus and Amor as the Greeks established between Aphrodite and Eros, the latter symbolising love and the former bodily pleasure.

Epicurus himself seems to have been nearly as hostile to Aphrodite as to Eros. But his disciples found in his works a good many statements which could be interpreted as more or less directly favourable to the goddess. He may have been ascetic enough personally. But he wrote: 'I spit upon moral principle and the hypocritical lip-service accorded to it, when no pleasure is to be derived therefrom.' He also asserted: 'The source and root of all that is good is the pleasure of the belly.' Such maxims, read with various degrees of understanding, had more influence on the subsequent 'Epicurean herd' than the master's own example.

Plutarch in his *Erotikos* (767 C–D) notes of Zeuxippus, one of the speakers introduced in that dialogue:

'Zeuxippus identified love with the unruly desire which tempts the soul to debauchery. He had not thought the matter out for himself. But he had often heard gloomy people who had never experienced love talk of it in this strain.'

I feel sure that Zeuxippus sympathised with the ideas of the Garden. His 'gloomy people who had never experienced love' were probably epicureans. Plutarch goes on:

'Some men of this type are attracted by the trifling dowries which certain unfortunate women may possess. Such husbands employ money and wives alike in household cares and sordid account-keeping. They quarrel with the poor wretches from morning till night and treat them like servants. Others, more interested in children than a wife, behave like the male grasshopper, which drops its seed on an onion or any other plant it comes across. They hastily fertilise the first body that comes their way, take what it produces and then bid farewell to marriage. Or, if they do allow it to continue, they pay no further attention to it whatever. For they are not interested in either loving or being loved.'

'The first body that comes their way' is exactly the same phrase as that used by Lucretius in the passage just quoted. The similarity of expression indicates a source common to both authors, which must be epicurean.

A little later in the *Erotikos* (769 F) Plutarch writes: 'The state of what is called "integral union" is truly that of a loving married couple. But the relations of persons who live together without any such solid bond of association recall the slight contacts and combinations mentioned by Epicurus' —in his description of the movements of atoms. 'They are characterised by collison and mutual repulsion and never acquire the unity which Love alone provides in presiding over the shared existence of husband and wife.'

It is no accident that Plutarch here designates loveless unions by an image borrowed from the atomic theory of epicurean physics, while he describes the fusion of loving hearts as 'integral union', a phrase first used by the Stoics, as we shall see immediately.

The Stoic theory of love appears to be a return to Plato's. For the philosophers of the Porch (*Stoa*) the sentiment was by no means only a carnal appetite. Its attachment to the worship of beauty, an impulse so deeply implanted in the Greek mind, aimed ultimately at a spiritual rather than physical conjunction.

The Stoics conceived of bodily beauty as a guarantee of moral excellence. Chrysippus in his essay *On Love* affirmed: 'Love is a part of friendship and is in no way to be disapproved. For beauty is the flower of virtue.' Another Stoic, Ariston of Chios, went so far as to declare: 'A virtuous and noble mind may be discerned in the bloom and grace of a body, just as a well-made shoe reveals the beauty of a foot.' Love aroused by a beautiful physique, regarded as an infallible index to moral beauty, 'must lead to virtue by the road of friendship'.

Such prescriptions recall the numerous arguments noted in Chapter 3 recommending pederasty as a method of education. Zeno, founder of the Porch school, and several of his successors, Chrysippus and Apollodorus for instance, did in fact defend homosexuality, which they regarded, however, as the prerogative of philosophers. In this matter, as in so much else, these first Stoics, who flourished in the third century B.C., defied the general social tendencies of their day. They were regarded as somewhat old-fashioned.

But the Stoics of a later date abandoned their theoretical support of pederasty and fervently championed normal sexual passion, especially that of husband and wife. Antipater of Tarsus writes in his essay *On Marriage*:

'Those who have neither wives nor children know nothing of true love. Other types of friendship or affection resemble mixtures of vegetables or similar objects which are merely juxtaposed, whereas the love of man and wife arises from the "integral union" typified by the mingling of water and wine.'

We saw above that Plutarch alludes to this Stoic idea of 'integral union' in his *Erotikos*. In his *Matrimonial Precepts* (44) he is undoubtedly inspired from a Stoic source when he observes:

'Philosophers have pointed out that while some things are composed of separate units, like fleets and armies, others are made of parts fastened to one another, like houses and ships, and still others of elements fused into a single entity, like living organisms. It is almost the same with the various kinds of marriage. Those arising from love eventually melt into perfect unity. Those contracted for the sake of a dowry or in order to have children are like a totality of components joined together. And those only undertaken to gratify sensuality resemble phenomena composed of separate units. . . . Just as physicians say that liquids mingle by integration'—i.e. even the smallest of their particles combine —'so husband and wife should form a single whole in which their bodies, their goods, their friends and their relatives all participate.'

The Cynics, philosophers of a popular stamp, with their

violent opinions and picturesque habits, have been called 'the Capuchins of Antiquity'. So far as theories of love are concerned, they seem to have developed on lines parallel with those of the Stoics. In the fourth century Antisthenes had said: 'If I met Aphrodite, I would strangle her with my own hands.' In the third century Crates of Thebes, one of Zeno's teachers, married Hipparchia, the sister of another Cynic philosopher, Metrocles. Hipparchia was of noble birth, very rich and very good-looking. She had many suitors. But she preferred Crates to them all, though he was extremely poor, for she admired his way of talking and his sober conduct. She became so fond of him that she herself turned philosopher and adopted the nomadic and austere habits of the Cynics. Diogenes Laertius included a notice of her in his *Lives of the Ancient Philosophers*. Later authors always cited the case of Crates and Hipparchia whenever the question whether a wise man should marry came under discussion.

The Cynic philosopher Dio Chrysostom, a contemporary of Plutarch, condemned all forms of dissipation. In his *Euboica* he gives a sympathetic account of family life among peasants, which he regards as the happiest and simplest mode of existence open to humanity.

Plutarch himself, writing in the last years of the first century A.D. and the first years of the second, benefited from the long tradition of philosophic thought, with its many and various aspects, anterior to his own day. Essentially a Platonist, he seems to a modern reader to stand half-way between the Academy as represented by Arcesilaus and the neo-platonism of Plotinus. On the subject of love, however, he sometimes abandons Plato's own views in order to adopt ideas originating in Aristotle's Lyceum or the Porch. But his development of all these theories is highly personal. He was not a builder of systems, but a psychologist and moralist. As metaphysician and theologian, too, he was quite capable of finding a way of his own through the immense jungle of Greek philosophic teaching.

The *Erotikos*, on which we have drawn so often in these pages, is a dialogue set in the Boeotian town of Thespiae, the only place in Greece where a special cult of Eros had been established. A temple dedicated to the Muses of Helicon stood near the city. Plutarch had arrived there, shortly after his marriage, in order to sacrifice to Eros during the festival, the *Erotideia*, in honour of the god. Naturally enough, a love-story, though rather a strange one, serves to introduce the dialogue. Ismenodora, a young local widow, wealthy and beautiful, is in love with the youth Bacchon, who has a number of admirers. The most persistent of these is Pisias, who joins in the conversation. It takes the form of a prolonged comparison of the two kinds of love, homosexual and heterosexual. This theme had frequently been dealt with since the appearance of Plato's *Symposium* and was again to be handled, after Plutarch's time, in the *Erotes*, a dialogue attributed to Lucian, and later still in a novel by Achilles Tatius entitled *Leucippe and Clitophon* (II, 34–8).

In the *Erotikos* the formal debate is cut short by Ismenodora herself, who takes the bold, even unprecedented, step of kidnapping young Bacchon as he passes her house on his way back from the arena. After this feat she persuades him to marry her. Such an event would of course have been unthinkable in the days of the classical ideal of female respectability.

Pisias and the other champions of homosexuality are naturally furious with the lady for her high-handed intervention. But a speaker on the opposite side, who evidently represents the author's views at this juncture, justifies her behaviour.

'Ismenodora,' he says, 'has hitherto led a most orderly life and never given any cause for scandal. It is clear that in this case she really acted under divine influence, a force more powerful than human reason.'

Her impulse could only have been directed by the erotic

form of *mania* described by Plato in the *Phaedo* as its highest and most beneficent manifestation.

But Plato had in mind exclusively homosexual love between males. Plutarch, as a good Platonist, uses for his dialogue in praise of love the arguments commonly employed by those who practised educational pederasty for the benefit of the objects of their affection. He had therefore to reconcile the traditional thought of the Academy with the *eros* inspired in Ismenodora by Bacchon and obviously reciprocated by the youth, since the dialogue ends with the celebration of their marriage.

Our author accordingly undertakes a task which would appear to a modern reader equivalent to breaking down an open door. He was impelled to it, however, by the deeply rooted convention of 'philosophic' homosexuality. Why, he asks, in effect, should not good-looking women be thought as capable as handsome young men of arousing passionate affection in the masculine mind? Why should not love for a girl or a matron be accorded the exceptional privileges enjoyed by the Platonic *eros*?

So far as is known, neither Aristotle nor the late Stoics embarked on so thoroughgoing a rehabilitation of heterosexuality. They thought they had done a good deal in allowing it access to the noble category of *philia*. A much longer step forward would have been taken if they had equated love of a woman with the Platonic *eros*, the sole condition and source of ultimate knowledge. Yet Plutarch did not hesitate to make this decisive advance.

The whole of the last part of the dialogue amounts to a defence of conjugal affection. It was undoubtedly inspired by the author's love for his wife Timoxena, by whom he had several children. She was most devoted to him. It is significant that he notes, at the very start of the dialogue, the arrival of both of them at Thespiae to offer sacrifice to the god of love in that city. Moreover, 'it was she who was to utter the prayer and perform the sacrifice.' The passage may well be thought to imply a discreet compliment to Timoxena, or rather perhaps a veiled dedication of the work to her.

A few lines may be quoted. They would seem commonplace enough as the product of a different civilisation. But they are surprising in the mouth of a Greek philosopher:

'Physical union with a wife initiates friendship. It resembles a common participation in great mysteries.'

The words *hieron megalon* in the *Erotikos* (769 A), incidentally, are strikingly analogous to those of St. Paul in the Epistle to the Ephesians (5, 32): 'This is a great mystery (*musterion mega*).' Yet it seems certain that Plutarch had not read the works of the Apostle and knew nothing whatever about Christianity. The *Erotikos* continues: 'The bodily pleasure experienced is brief. But it is like a seed giving rise to the daily growth between man and wife of mutual respect, kindness, affection and confidence. The Delphians were right to name Aphrodite "Harmony" and Homer was justified in calling such a union "friendship". . . . Wives love their children and their husband. The emotional power they thus acquire becomes a fertile soil, ready to receive the seed of love, and is richly endowed with a variety of attractions and beauties. . . . In marriage, to love is a greater advantage than to be loved. For, in loving, one is not affected by anything which might otherwise spoil or interfere with the bond of matrimony. . . . The love of a virtuous woman knows no autumn. It retains its vigour even when white hairs and wrinkles come. In fact, it lasts until death.'

Plutarch seeks to illustrate his pronouncements by proving that conjugal fidelity in women may amount to heroism. He relates the touching and dramatic stories of Camma and Empona. These women were not, however, Greeks. They were Celts, the former from Galatia and the latter from Gaul. It is implied, perhaps, that the nation had in those days a special reputation for virtue of this kind. We shall return to this subject in the following chapter.

L. Dugas (*L'Amitié antique* etc., Alcan, 1894, pp. 142–50,

passim) seems to me to have given an excellent account of Plutarch's contribution to the philosophy of love. We may therefore end our examination of this field with some extracts from the work in question.

'Plutarch's originality consists in his discovery that conjugal affection is the highest form of love. . . . He confers upon heterosexuality the fruits of Plato's triumphant progress in the moral domain. He assigns to normal lovers a distant aim of mystical and deeply promising character. His theory sums up the ideas of antiquity concerning love and takes them to their logical conclusion. His tone and emphasis, his recollections of former notions and his involuntary returns to the prejudices which his own views replace, are all of his time. But his thought anticipates our own by his formulation of the problem and the basis of his concepts. . . . If we assume that Plato and the Stoics were idealists, Aristotle and Epicurus realists, Plutarch may be regarded as reconciling the two attitudes. While he cannot imagine love in isolation from the satisfaction of lust and is entirely opposed to pederasty, he ascribes to the "legitimate" love of man and wife the heroic virtues which all antiquity had reserved exclusively for homosexual affection. He thus established a principle from which the ideal of chivalrous love was to emerge.'

7

ROMANTIC LOVE

'Daphnis, swear to me upon your herd and by the goat which suckled you that you will never desert Chloe.'

LONGUS.

To use the phrase 'romantic love' in relation to the ancient Greeks is to employ a term which had no place in their language, any more than the word 'romance'. They were of course well acquainted with fictional narrative, in the form of 'myths', which Plato and so many others after him recounted as illustrations of their ideas or merely in order to interest and attract their readers by a 'good story'. Neither ancient nor modern Greeks have ever been short of creative imagination. But the 'romance', though related to the 'myth', is not quite the same thing, since it deals with the lives and actions of a number of characters, including primarily a hero and heroine in love with each other.

The word 'romance' may be modern. But its meaning is ancient. For the Greeks have left us several such long pieces of fiction, in which historical personages sometimes appear. We cannot call such works today anything but 'romances'. The name fits them perfectly. And we shall soon see that 'romantic love' also describes with great precision the conception underlying most of these productions.

The story of Helen, as told in a few scattered lines of the *Iliad*, is itself romantic, with the added pungency of a broken marriage. For Helen does not cease to love Menelaus, 'the husband of her youth', and their daughter Hermione. But Aphrodite throws her, like a plaything, into the arms of the handsome Paris. Then comes her abduction, followed by a bitter-sweet captivity and, at last, after long years, return to the hearth she had deserted. The novelists of the last epoch of ancient Greek literature often evoked the enchanting image of Helen, the prototype, for beauty at least, of all their heroines.

But the *Iliad*, after all, treats more of war than love. The *Odyssey* may plausibly be considered the first Greek 'romance', or at any rate 'romantic epic', as we noted in Chapter 1. It was only after an ordeal of twenty years, those of the war and his prolonged voyage home, that Ulysses again beheld his beloved wife Penelope. He had never forgotten her, in spite of the charmers with whom he had dallied at certain ports of call. She for her part had remained resolutely loyal to him in both body and soul, disdaining every importunity of her suitors.

In Chapter 2, dealing with mythology, we also recalled several dramatic stories of love and death, such as those of Orpheus and Eurydice, Protesilaus and Laodamia, Alcestis and Admetus, together with the legends of Bellerophon, Perseus and Tereus. The last-named has been called a 'gloomy tale'. For Tereus violates his sister-in-law and cuts out her tongue, but cannot escape the fatal consequences of his lust. On the other hand, 'edification' characterises the account of the most beautiful of the daughters of Danaus, who loved her young husband too much to carry out the cruel order of her father to kill him. P. Grimal is therefore quite correct in stating that 'the romance can be found in outline at every stage of the development of a myth'.

Herodotus has been called the Father of History. But he also provides an endless stream of absolutely incredible 'good stories', like that of Rhampsinitus (11, 121), the Pharaoh who placed his own daughter in a brothel in order to lay hands on a clever thief who had been robbing him. But the monarch eventually conceived such an admiration for the fellow's ingenuity that he gave him the same daughter in marriage! In view of the experiences the girl had undergone at her father's command this tale is more like a detective story than a romance. And in fact the modern writer Alexandre Arnoux plagiarised it after his own fashion in *Les Rêveries d'un Policier amateur.*

Herodotus also relates (VI, 61) that a certain little Spartan girl, who was very ugly, was taken every day by her nurse to a chapel dedicated to Helen of Troy. For it was hoped that the child's looks might be improved by prayer to that deified heroine. One day a woman, no doubt Helen herself, encountered the pair and stroked the little girl's head. Instantly the child became the prettiest in the country. When she grew up and married, her husband's best friend fell violently in love with her. But he was more astute than Paris. Instead of carrying her off he employed a cunning ruse to force her legitimate spouse to hand her over. The friend was no other than Ariston, King of Sparta, whose stratagem, as reported by Herodotus, we described in Chapter 4.

In ancient Greek literature the first piece of prose fiction of any considerable length is Xenophon's *Cyropaedia.* It is essentially the portrait of an ideal monarch. But in Books V and VI an edifying romance, that of Panthea, wife of Abradates, King of Susiana, is narrated. She was captured by Cyrus, who treated her with respect, though she was very beautiful, and entrusted her to the care of one of his friends, the Mede Araspes, who boasted that he was perfectly capable of controlling his passions. 'Love,' he told Cyrus, 'depends upon will. One only loves a person whom one wishes to love.' Cyrus felt some doubt about this statement. And it turned out that he was right. For his friend, despite these lofty claims, soon fell in love with the fair captive and, when she resolutely repulsed his advances, threatened her with violence. When this development was reported to Cyrus, he made arrangements for Panthea to be restored to her husband. 'They immediately fell into each other's arms with all the joy that attends unexpected good fortune.'

Abradates, touched by the generosity of Cyrus, became his faithful ally.

While the *Odyssey* may be regarded as a romantic epic, it was Euripides who wrote the first romantic tragedies. In the *Hippolytus* and the *Medea* he showed himself one of the greatest and most realistic authors ever to portray the passion of love. Aristotle called him 'the most tragic of all poets'. But he did not hesitate to treat the legends he interpreted in his own way, introducing into his plots pathetic and dramatic incidents, unexpected encounters and sudden recognitions. Such elements in his work render him the direct predecessor of the New Comedy and the Greek novel.

In one of his lost plays Merope recognises her son at the last moment, when she is about to kill him. Ion, the young hero of the surviving tragedy bearing his name, is a foundling, the son of Apollo and Creusa, an Athenian woman. He is employed as a ministrant at the temple of Delphi, which his mother visits. She speaks to him without recognising him. Then, believing him to be an illegitimate son of her husband, she tries to poison him. Ion is about to have her put to death when the oracle proclaims the truth.

According to H. Grégoire, who has edited this play, both the tragi-comedies of Euripides and the subsequent New Comedy are full of 'seductions, abandoned offspring, recognitions by rings, necklaces or playthings, the desperation of deserted mistresses, spilt blood crying for vengeance, maternal and filial tenderness, devoted or melancholy sentimentality and loyal, self-sacrificing slaves'.

The comedies of Menander and his Greek rivals were imitated again and again by Plautus and Terence. These plays bear hardly any resemblance to those of Aristophanes. For they are based almost entirely upon amorous intrigue and romance.

L. Bodin and P. Mazon state:

'The subject of Menander's comedies seems to have been, as a general rule, thwarted love. A young man, for instance,

is attracted by a foreign girl of dubious social position. His
father wishes him to marry someone else. Then it is suddenly
discovered that the girl is a freeborn citizen. She had been
abandoned in infancy by her parents and is recognised by
the ornaments she had worn as a child. Such is the simplest
form of plot. It is varied in all sorts of ways. But the action is
nearly always motivated by a secret love and a new-born
infant whose paternity has to be proved respectable. For
example, a girl has been ravished by a stranger during a
nocturnal revel. She gives birth to a child which is immediately abandoned. The mother then marries her seducer
without recognising him. He learns by chance of his wife's
previous disgrace and leaves her. But later he is himself
recognised as the father of the child.'

This is the plot of Menander's *Arbitration*, to which we
referred in Chapter 4. The authors of the above passage
continue:

'It is very doubtful whether such situations occurred with
any frequency at Athens in the fourth century. The behaviour
of a society as a whole cannot be deduced from its drama.
For playwrights do not handle the ordinary events of
contemporary life, but those most calculated to arouse the
particular emotions common to the masses of their day. We
can only say that the custom of exposing infants with articles
by which they might be identified at a later date had
occasionally brought about their recognition in unforeseen,
strange or touching circumstances, which had excited
popular interest.'

The love-affairs dealt with in all such comedies might
involve either a courtesan or a girl of free birth. But the
latter might often be supposed to be socially inferior to the
lover or even a slave. The occasion on which the young man
falls in love is frequently that of a festival. For, as already
noted, virgins did not appear in public except when participating in ceremonies, especially those of a religious nature.

When the piece begins, affairs are always at a crisis.

Sometimes the heroine is cruel and won't open her door. Others are kept locked up by tyrannical masters. The girls are then the object of nocturnal serenades, secret visits and 'closed-door elegies'. It is often necessary to bribe a maid-servant or a male guardian in order to obtain access to the beloved young woman.

Xenarchus, one of the comic poets, gives a list of the plans open to the wooer of someone else's wife. He will have to climb stealthily up a ladder, or make his way into the house through a hole in the roof or hidden in a truss of straw. Abductions were by no means rare, with or without the lady's consent. Paris had plenty of imitators.

Rivals both male and female sometimes have violent quarrels and come to blows. But as a rule gentler methods of persuasion are adopted, by resorting to bribes of money and gifts. Occasionally two young men who are both after the same girl agree to draw lots for her.

Jealousy and resentment in love may be represented by altercations and harsh treatment of the offender or by recourse to sorcery, as we noticed in Chapter 5, where courtesans were in question. Lovers' tiffs recur regularly. But they are usually due to misunderstandings which are cleared up in the end.

Young men are sometimes victimised by a pimp, a pro-curess or a courtesan, who fleece them. Shortage of cash being always disastrous to progress in love, they resort to all sorts of expedients to escape from the toils of poverty. For the most part such tricks have to be kept dark and come perilously close to fraud.

Disguises are frequently assumed. In one play a youth dresses up as a newly wedded wife.

The habitual opposition of fathers to their sons' plans, coupled with the ensuing lack of funds, accounts for many and varied episodes. Sometimes a father tries to have the woman who is ruining his son done away with. Or he may employ every possible method of persuading her to break with her lover. His last card is to force his son into instant marriage with a girl of the father's own choice. The son may meet this bolt from the blue by promising to do everything he is asked, so as to gain time.

Married men may also be found pursuing love-affairs away from home. Their chief concern is then to prevent their frolics being discovered.

In short, an almost infinite variety of situations is exploited by the New Comedy in its incessant search for a fresh approach to the eternal theme of love rejected or, if reciprocated, thwarted by circumstances.

We can no longer accept today the theory of Erwin Rohde, a German historian of the Greek novel, who maintained that this form of literature arose in the second and third centuries A.D. from the artificial blend of two previous categories of composition, love-stories as narrated in the Alexandrine elegy and travellers' tales. But it is quite true that the poetry of the Hellenistic epoch was a further strong influence, following those of Homer, Euripides and the New Comedy, on the Greek conception of romantic love.

In Chapter 4 we mentioned Alexandrine poetry in connection with the improved respect accorded at that period to women and the affection they inspire. A few further considerations only need be added here, or rather a glance at two love-stories which may be regarded as typical of those treated by the poets in question.

The melancholy tale of Hero and Leander is known to us from a few epigrams in the Greek Anthology. The events may be summarised as follows. At Abydos on the coast of Asia Minor there lived a young man named Leander, in love with a priestess of Aphrodite named Hero, who lived at Sestos in Thrace, just across the Hellespont (the modern Dardanelles) from Abydos. Every evening Leander swam across the strait, guided by a lamp which Hero lit on the top of a tower of the house in which she lived. But one stormy night the lamp went out. In the darkness Leander could not find the shore. Next day the tide washed his corpse to the foot of Hero's tower. Unwilling to survive the death of her lover, she flung herself down and perished.

According to L. Sechan (*Lettres d'humanité*, XII, 1953, p. 26), 'the Roman poets also took an interest in this story. The *Heroides* of Ovid, in particular, include two letters supposed to have been exchanged by the lovers across the waters that separated them. Their tragedy was not cast in dramatic form by the ancients. But in modern times it inspired some notable lines by Schiller and a fine play by Grillparzer.'

The tale of Acontius and Cydippe was included by Callimachus in his *Origines*, ('Causes'), a long collection of poems in elegiac metre, but going into almost as much detail as would prose fiction. Unfortunately only a few fragments, found on papyrus, have survived. But one of the *Letters* of Aristaenetus gives an outline of the whole affair which is worth relating.

A very handsome youth named Acontius lived in the island of Ceos. He was courted by a number of male lovers. 'Many who loved him threw the *cottabus*, in the Sicilian manner, from the bottoms of their wine-cups.' His family was respectable, but of limited means. While on a visit to the holy island of Delos for the annual festival he saw a most beautiful girl in the temple of Artemis and instantly fell in love with her. She was an Athenian citizen named Cydippe.

Acontius conceived the idea of cutting a solemn declaration on an apple which would automatically betroth the girl to him. Apples, as we saw in Chapter 5, were traditionally regarded as the most significant of a lover's gifts. The inscription read, 'I swear by Artemis to marry only Acontius.' He threw the apple to the girl, who was sitting with her nurse. The latter picked up the apple and gave it to Cydippe, who innocently read the inscription aloud. Thus she involuntarily bound herself by oath to Acontius.

At this point in the story the chief surviving fragment by

Callimachus begins. Cydippe's father knew nothing of what had occurred at Delos. He made preparations for her marriage to another man. But the day before the ceremony was due to take place 'the girl grew deadly pale. The malady we call holy set her at death's door. Again the nuptial couch was made ready. Again the bride fell ill, for seven months, of a quartan ague. A third time arrangements were considered for her wedding. For the third time a dread fit of shuddering seized Cydippe. Her father did not await a fourth. He set sail for Delphi, to consult the oracle of Phoebus. The god, by night, replied: "An oath sworn in the name of Artemis prevents your daughter's marriage. My sister ... was at Delos when your daughter swore that she would have no other husband but Acontius. I advise you to fulfil to the letter your daughter's oath." Thus spake the god. The father returned home and questioned Cydippe, who told him all that had happened. . . . The deity thus enforced the keeping of the promise and amid the wedding chants sung by the maidenly companions of the bride her marriage was at once celebrated. Acontius, on the night when thou didst loose her virginal girdle thou wouldst not have bartered it against the wealth of Midas. All who have known the cruelties of the god of love bear witness to the truth of my words.'

Like this tale, some others preserved on fragments of papyrus are only known to us in part. For example, a papyrus of the first century A.D. notes of the Assyrian king Ninus:

'At seventeen he fell in love with a girl of fourteen'—she was perhaps Semiramis—'and in order to gain her admiration performed some remarkable feats. He went to war against the Armenians. . . . Proud of this exploit, he tried to win over his mother, who opposed his wish to marry the girl he loved ... who longed to be his wife.'

Plutarch, however, gives quite a different version of the affair between Ninus and Semiramis (*Erotikos* 753 D–E.): 'Semiramis, a Syrian, was the female attendant and concubine of a slave born in the palace of King Ninus. That mighty ruler noticed her one day and fell madly in love with her. She eventually acquired so much influence over him that she demanded and received his permission to reign over the kingdom for a day, seated upon his throne and wearing the royal diadem. Ninus ordered all his subjects to serve and obey her as they would himself. The first commands she issued were not oppressive, for she wished to test the docility of the guards. But when she found that they did not protest she ordered them to seize the person of the king, then to bind him and finally to kill him. After this murder she reigned long over Asia with great pomp.'

Some of the stories illustrated the condign punishments meted out by Aphrodite and her son Eros, according to legend, to cruel and callous women. One such was the Cretan Gorgo. But a gap in the manuscript of Plutarch's *Erotikos* (766 D) leaves us in ignorance of the result of her behaviour. Then there was the Cyprian Anaxarete, known as 'she who leans from the window' (*parakyptusa*). The youth Iphis was in love with her. But she disdained him. In his despair he hanged himself at her door. Yet his suicide left her so indifferent that when his funeral procession passed her house she appeared at her window to watch with interest the crowds which had assembled on that tragic occasion. Thereupon Aphrodite, angered by the girl's inhumanity, changed her to stone in the very attitude of leaning from the window. The statue was then lodged in a temple at Salamis in Cyprus. It is quite probable that the unusual posture of the image gave rise to the story.

But such tales were exceptional. The majority of those preserved celebrate, on the contrary, the tenderness and fidelity, amounting at times to heroism, of wives to husbands. Naturally enough Plutarch, the champion of conjugal affection in his *Erotikos*, relates a good many anecdotes of this kind, both in that work and in his brief dissertations entitled *The Virtue of Women* and *Love Stories*.

Camma, the wonderfully beautiful wife of the Galatian

chief Sinat, was beloved by another chief named Sinorix. But, finding her resolutely faithful to her husband, he murdered Sinat. The widow retired to serve as priestess in a temple of Artemis. When Sinorix visited her there, she consented to receive him. She pretended to accept the proposal of marriage which he made to her. Then, as though to confirm the agreement by a solemn libation, 'she led him by the hand to the altar of the goddess. On it stood a cup of mead which she had previously mixed with poison. She poured a few drops from the cup, then drank half the liquid which remained and handed the goblet to Sinorix, who drank off the contents. Then she uttered a loud cry of joy, called upon Sinat by name and said: "Beloved husband, it was only in expectation of this day that I endured the pain of life without thee. Rejoice now, for I am about to rejoin thee after taking vengeance upon this infamous scoundrel, whose death I am as glad to share as I was to share thy life." Sinorix, borne away upon a litter, expired shortly afterwards. Camma survived for the rest of that day and the following night. Then she died, they say, in perfect serenity and happiness.'

Another very affecting story also refers to a Celtic wife, Empona or Epponina of Gaul, married to Sabinus, who was associated with Civilis in the revolt against Rome of 69 A.D. But this anecdote is probably true, being mentioned by Tacitus (*Histories*, IV, 67), and cannot therefore be cited as an example of the Greek conception of love. Nevertheless, Plutarch gives it a place of honour at the end of his *Erotikos*, thus proving that he regarded it as a significant instance of conjugal fidelity. He was also personally acquainted, it appears, with one of Empona's sons.

Plutarch's five *Love Stories* are concerned chiefly with crimes due to amorous passion and rivalry. We shall quote only that relating to the Boeotian Aristoclea. A young woman of striking beauty, she had two suitors, Straton and Callisthenes.

'Straton was the richer of the two and also the more passionately in love with the girl, having seen her bathing in the Hercynian spring at Lebadea before going to carry her basket of offerings in a religious procession.'

Aristoclea's father could not make up his mind between the rivals and decided to abide by the decision of an oracle, that of Trophonius. But Straton, confident of his success, demanded that Aristoclea herself should settle the question. She, however, chose Callisthenes. Straton then conspired with friends to set an ambush on the road which the girl would have to take to reach a certain spring where a rite preliminary to the marriage ceremony was to be performed. She was escorted by Callisthenes and his party. In the ensuing conflict for possession of Aristoclea's person she was herself fatally injured and Straton, flinging himself on her corpse, committed suicide.

The tale of Eros (Cupid) and Psyche, briefly referred to in Chapter 2, is much more original and interesting. Its author is Apuleius, a Roman who knew Hellas and its literature very well. But in all probability the legend was invented by a Greek. It is one of the most charming left to us by the writers of antiquity. One of the sentences reads: 'Apollo, though he was a Greek and an Ionian at that, had the courtesy to reply with an oracle in Latin when consulted by the author of our Milesian Tale.' This pleasantry seems to prove that Apuleius was indebted to a Greek source.

Psyche was a king's daughter, the youngest of three sisters. She was so beautiful that she was worshipped like a goddess. Jealous Aphrodite ordered her son Eros to punish so impertinent a rival. An oracle pronounced by Apollo of Miletus decreed that Psyche should be abandoned on a rock in the mountains. But the gentle breeze Zephyr wafted her away from the rock and put her down on a flowery meadow in a deep valley. She soon found a wonderful palace close by, where invisible attendants ministered to her least desires.

A mysterious stranger who only visited her at night and in

darkness rendered her pregnant. He warned her against her two sisters, who were jealous of her and meant to do her harm. But Psyche, who was still fond of them, nevertheless contrived to receive them. They gradually acquired an influence over her and eventually convinced her that the lover she had never seen was a horrible monster. Although he had forbidden her to light a lamp, she did so, and was about to strike him with it, when she perceived that he was Eros, the god of love, in the full splendour of his divinity. Then a drop of oil fell from the lamp upon his shoulder and he immediately flew away.

Psyche was thereupon forced by Aphrodite to undergo a series of dreadful ordeals, too long to describe here. But meanwhile Eros, cured of his burn, at last succeeded in persuading Zeus to confer immortality upon Psyche and permit him to marry her. The daughter born to them was named Pleasure.

The story undoubtedly preserves traces of such ancient figures of folklore as 'Prince Charming' and 'Beauty and the Beast'. But it certainly also seems to have been conceived to illustrate the Platonic myth of Love and the Soul, referred to in Chapter 6, the word *psyche* being the Greek for 'soul'.

In order to reach the divine realm which is the soul's true habitation she must be attracted thither by love. She must also repudiate all earthly affections and all the burdens which weigh her down to this world. Further, she must suffer a long series of purifying trials before attaining to the eternal delight of the 'blessed vision'.

The *Cupid and Psyche* of Apuleius is a fanciful composition, a kind of fairytale. The Greek novelists are as a rule more realistic, without troubling themselves much about probability. Their details are often exact, picturesque and shrewdly observed. But the plot as a whole piles one incredible incident on another.

G. Dalmeyda has given a good definition of this curious and fascinating species of literature.

'The Greek novel, in a word, is an epic of decadent type, using obvious methods to promote interest. Good and bad characters are set in opposition, the benevolent against intrusive "third parties". The attractive personages are afflicted by storm and shipwreck, or attacks by brigands or pirates. A danger no less formidable resides in the exceptional and disastrous physical beauty of both hero and heroine. The moment they appear people of both sexes fall in love with them, displaying equal ardour but more or less humanity and delicacy in the process. . . . These various misfortunes all serve to postpone the union of the protagonists and sometimes seem likely to render it for ever impossible. The novel therefore describes a pursuit delayed by obstacles. A malevolent fate incessantly retards the consummation so devoutly desired by the couple.'

As the Greek novels are all love-stories, their titles are simply the names of the pair whose mutual affection and woes lend drama to the narrative, for instance Chaereas and Callirhoe, Habrocomes and Anthea (or The Ephesians), Daphnis and Chloe, Theagenes and Chariclea (or The Ethiopians), Leucippe and Clitophon.

The first, *Chaereas and Callirhoe*, seems to have been composed some time in the first century B.C. Chariton, the author, was an Asian Greek, born at Aphrodisias in Caria. He gave his tale a fairly accurate historical setting. But he took considerable liberties with chronology. On the whole his world is that of Greek civilisation at the end of the fifth century B.C. The action moves from Syracuse, where the first citizen is the general Hermocrates, who defeated the Athenian expedition against Sicily, to Miletus and Babylon, where Artaxerxes is king, and then to Phoenicia, Cyprus and back again to Syracuse.

The novel is a regular 'lovers' epic', chock full of quotations from Homer. But it is dedicated to the glory, not of heroes like Achilles and Ulysses, but of beauty as personified by the Syracusan Callirhoe, daughter of Hermocrates. We

may recall that Callirhoe ('fair-flowing') was the name
of the spring at Athens from which water was fetched to
bathe a bride before marriage. But Chariton seems only
to feel hostility towards the Athenians. His 'epic', like
Homer's, mentions numerous interventions by a deity. But
the latter is always Aphrodite, no longer Zeus, Athena or
Apollo.

Callirhoe, then, was 'a girl of wondrous beauty, admired
by all Sicily, for she seemed not human but divine. Her
loveliness was not simply that of nereid or nymph, but of
Aphrodite while yet a virgin.' Wherever she went, in fact,
men instantly fell in love with her at first sight. Even the King
of Persia did so. This fatal privilege was also Helen's. But
Callirhoe could only love once. She remained steadfastly
loyal to Chaereas at heart, although circumstances obliged
her to make a second marriage.

When her mother took her for the first time to the festival
of Aphrodite at Syracuse, she was seen by Chaereas on his
way home from the gymnasium. The eyes of the young
couple met. In a flash they each knew they were in love for
life. They married and were happy. But their happiness did
not last. For happy pairs, it is said, have no history and
Chariton's long novel is only just beginning.

For other men, who loved Callirhoe in vain, slandered her
to her husband. Their sinister insinuations made so much
impression on him that in a fit of rage he actually kicked his
beloved wife, who was pregnant, at a spot between thorax
and abdomen. His violence led to a long series of unexpected
happenings. Callirhoe fainted. She appeared to be dead and
was buried. But robbers who broke into the tomb were
terrified to see her move. They recovered sufficiently,
however, to carry her off on their ship to Ionia, where she
was sold to Dionysius, the richest man in Miletus. He first
sees her in a chapel of Aphrodite and instantly falls helplessly
in love with her. He proposes marriage. At first she refuses
him with abhorrence. Then she remembers that she is about

to bear the child of Chaereas. At last, after fearful struggles with her conscience and prolonged hesitations, she agrees. But, although Dionysius is very good to her, she remains in her heart devoted solely to her absent first husband.

He has already left Syracuse aboard a trireme in search of his wife, whose tomb had been found empty. But the ship is captured by pirates and he is himself sold as a slave in Caria, where he has to work terribly hard and is nearly crucified. As a result of complicated intrigues the satrap of Caria, who is also in love with Callirhoe, and Dionysius the Milesian are summoned to Babylon by the Great King to stand their trial. Callirhoe hears that Chaereas is dead. The news is false. But she erects a cenotaph at Miletus in memory of him, exclaiming, 'Each of us has now buried the other!'

Egypt then rebels against Persia. Chaereas joins the insurgents and greatly distinguishes himself in the war. At the head of a fleet he sweeps the Persians from the sea and captures Arados, where the Persian king had installed his own wife and all his attendants, including Callirhoe herself. But Chaereas does not know that she is among his female Persian prisoners. Further intervention by Aphrodite is required to bring about a happy ending. For the goddess had now changed her mind. She had formerly been extremely annoyed with Chaereas 'because of his untimely jealously and because, after receiving from her the most splendid of gifts, such as even Paris had not obtained, he had requited her favour with violence.' But now she is sorry for him, since he has so 'amply atoned for his offence against love by his wanderings from west to east in the midst of a thousand torments.' She accordingly arranges for the lovers, after her long persecution of them, to meet again. 'I think,' the author adds amiably, 'that this last Book will please readers, for it will make them forget the calamitous events of the first Books.'

At this final reunion of the lovers Chaereas and Callirhoe each faint three times running. Then, after having had their fill of tears and the exchange of news, they embrace and 'rejoice in the restoration of the conjugal rights they had known in former days.' This quotation from the *Odyssey* (XXIII, 295) confirms the fact, if proof is still needed, that Chariton's novel was inspired by the famous tale of Ulysses and Penelope.

Callirhoe offers up a final prayer to Aphrodite in which, however, she does not mention her son, who is being brought up at Miletus by Dionysius in the belief that the child is his own. It is true that she has already written to ask him to provide the boy with a wife as soon as he is grown up and send him to Syracuse. But Callirhoe is evidently much more of a loving wife than a mother, as indeed the convention of the Greek novel demands.

We have considered this example of it at some length as being very probably the oldest in existence and revealing with special clarity the Greek notion of romantic love. The idea is illustrated by the adventures of a young man and a girl, both of great physical beauty and elevation of mind, who pass through many devastating experiences and yet remain entirely loyal in spirit to each other. No reference to homosexuality can be found in the novel, except at one point, where Callirhoe says to Chaereas, 'Your marriage is a great affliction to your lovers.' Moreover, Eros is replaced by Aphrodite throughout the work. Chariton thus abandons the distinction drawn by philosophers between the goddess of erotic pleasure and the god of erotic sentiment. For he represents his lovers, in their mutual attachment, as bound equally by the flesh and the spirit. Yet he remains thoroughly Greek in regarding beauty as a gift from the gods, at once the most precious and the most dangerous of all possessions. Many scenes, especially that of Callirhoe's arrival in Babylon, when a sort of beauty contest takes place between her and a Persian woman named Rodogune, throw into strong relief the extraordinary power, which appears miraculous, of youth combined with flawless physique.

Xenophon of Ephesus, author of *The Ephesians*, may have lived in the second century A.D. He was inspired to a great extent both by the story of Acontius and Cydippe as recounted by Callimachus and by Chariton's novel. The young Ephesian Habrocomes is a 'masterpiece of beauty', and also of virtue. But he is very proud of himself and disdainful of other people.

'He even refused to regard Eros himself as a god, scornfully dismissing him and holding him of no account. No one, he said, would ever fall in love or submit to that false god except intentionally. Whenever he saw a chapel or statuette of Eros, he jeered at it, declaring that there was no Eros who was not inferior to himself in beauty.'

Eros made Habrocomes pay dearly for his insolent contempt, just as Aphrodite, in the tragedy by Euripides, punished Hippolytus for disdaining her in his youthful pride.

The jealous god accordingly proceeds to chastise the sixteen-year-old lad by making him fall in love. At the festival of Artemis, chief goddess of the Ephesians, the procession of virgins is headed by Anthea, aged fourteen.

'She resembled a flower in bodily beauty and her attire added to her grace. . . . More than once the Ephesians, seeing her in the sacred enclosure, had offered her divine honours, mistaking her for Artemis.'

As soon as the boy and girl saw each other they were enslaved by love, for such was the will of Eros. Both, when they returned home, 'beheld each other again in thought and the fire of love burned within them'.

Thereupon the two young people fell ill. They were soon almost at death's door. Their fathers consulted the god at Colophon and heard an oracle foretelling the future tribulations of the lovers. Nevertheless, they were married and soon 'enjoyed together the pleasures of Aphrodite'. But their parents conceived the disastrous idea of sending them to Egypt for their honeymoon. After the ship had called at

Rhodes Phoenician pirates seized it. The terrible ordeal prophesied by the oracle began.

'They fell into all kinds of traps laid by pirates, brigands, slave-dealers and, above all, men and women inflamed by their irresistible beauty. They were separated, never ceased their efforts to find each other and risked their lives continually, preferring death to disloyalty and even in the worst extremities determined to preserve their chastity. Their resolute virtue triumphed over the most menacing dangers and gave them, in the end, complete victory.'

As G. Dalmeyda notes, this novel certainly celebrates 'the heroic mutual fidelity of husband and wife'.

The Ephesians is particularly remarkable for its continuously edifying and pious tone, amounting almost to mysticism. It deals less with passion than with virtue, the quality which, after successfully overcoming many trials, is assured of happiness both here and in the next world. For the author makes several allusions to the blissful immortality which awaits his protagonists, since they have always been ready to sacrifice their earthly lives to their constancy in love. Like Stoic sages, in fact, this model pair would rather commit suicide than survive their only reason for living, their love for each other. But the novel must of course go on to its happy ending. So the helping hand of the author invariably rescues them at the very last moment from destruction.

Longus, who wrote the famous pastoral romance, *Daphnis and Chloe*, seems to have lived, like Xenophon of Ephesus, in the second century A.D. According to P. Grimal, the novel by Longus is 'a brief work, notable for its unity of place and theme, the subject being simply the discovery of love by two young and chaste persons. The tale is essentially a rustic idyll in prose. As in a typical idyll by Theocritus the description of emotions is balanced by that of ordinary rural life. . . . It is more of a short story than a novel.' We may add that the treatment is distinctly licentious and erotic, a fact which no doubt partly accounts for the celebrity of the tale.

For the Greek novel is highly versatile. It may describe either an exclusive and almost mystical type of love or mere carnality adorned with an abundance of improper detail, as in *Lucius or the Ass*, a work attributed to Lucian. But as this last production is not strictly speaking a love-story, we shall not refer to it.

Longus writes a foreword to his book, a kind of dedication of it to Love, the Nymphs and Pan, god of shepherds.

'He who has loved will be reminded by it of his love and he who has never loved will be initiated by it into love. For there can be no one at all who either has escaped or should escape love, while beauty exists and men keep their eyes open.'

In the Lesbian countryside near Mytilene, where Sappho once lived, a couple of shepherds find two children whose parents have abandoned them. The boy is being suckled by a goat. He is dressed in a purple cloak with a golden clasp and has a toy sword with an ivory hilt. An ewe is suckling the little girl. She wears a headband embroidered with gold thread, gilded shoes and golden anklets. These articles eventually enable the children to be identified as belonging to wealthy families. The shepherds called the boy Daphnis and the girl Chloe.

The children are set to watch the flocks and herds of the rustics who adopt them. When the boy is fifteen and the girl thirteen they begin, in perfect innocence, to love each other, though they know nothing of love. But an old cowman named Philetas tells them about Eros. Soon they are exchanging solemn declarations of eternal love. All the sterotyped phrases crop up. When Daphnis sets out in the snow for Chloe's house, barely one and a quarter miles distant, the author gravely observes that 'love knows no barriers, neither fire nor water nor Scythian snows.' When the couple meet after a few weeks of separation 'they almost dropped to the ground in their emotion.' They talk such typical twaddle as 'Courage, Daphnis, the sun is warm!'

'Ah, Chloe, if it could only be as warm as the fire that burns my heart!'

The innocent pair, though reciprocating each other's love and enjoying perfect freedom in the open fields, do not manage to consummate their desires. There is a reference to pederasty in the attempt of the parasite Gnatho to seduce Daphnis. Moreover, the latter is given a 'lesson in love' by an obliging girl named Lycenium, who is quite satisfied with her experiment. Nevertheless, Chloe remains a virgin, simply because the convention of this type of fiction requires physical union to follow, not to precede, marriage. Daphnis, of course, finds his parents again. Then Chloe finds hers. Both families belong to the Mytilenean aristocracy. At last the marriage of the protagonists, after being delayed by adventures too numerous to describe here, takes place 'and Daphnis acted as he had been instructed by Lycenium. Then Chloe, for the first time, understood that their former diversions in the woods had been merely shepherds' frolics.'

The novel entitled *Theagenes and Chariclea*, also called *The Ethiopians*, was written by a certain Heliodorus, probably in the third century A.D. He appears to have been at one time a Priest of the Sun at Emesa in Syria and then, after his conversion to Christianity, Bishop of Tricca in Thessaly. After all, there is no reason why a future bishop should not have written a love-story in his youth!

Anyhow, the work is of a chaste and edifying character, like *The Ephesians*, with a great deal in it about priests and sanctuaries. Amyot's translation of 1547 had a profound influence on European literature for two hundred years. Racine read it while at school in Port Royal at the age of fifteen. When his master confiscated the book the boy told him coolly that its loss did not worry him, as he knew it by heart. The statement was certainly an exaggeration, for *The Ethiopians* is very long. Nevertheless, the future author of *Phèdre* and *Bajazet* was undoubtedly much indebted to it, though P. Grimal perhaps exaggerates in his turn when he writes: 'Heliodorus was in truth a great revelation to Racine, having first introduced him to the exciting inspiration of the pagan world, so long mysterious to him.' Racine, however, soon read many other works of Greek literature of more merit than the novel by Heliodorus, beginning with Homer and Euripides.

The Ethiopians differs from the productions of Chariton and Xenophon in dealing with a betrothed, not a married, couple. They do not marry until the end of the story, after many a narrow escape from death and an even worse fate, which threatened on several occasions to cause them to break their oaths of fidelity by entering upon forced unions with other lovers.

Chariclea is the daughter of Hydaspes, King of Ethiopia, and his wife Persinna. But the infant's skin is white. For Persinna, when the child was conceived, had been looking at a picture representing Perseus releasing the nude Andromeda from the rock to which she had been bound. 'The seed in her womb,' writes the author, 'had assumed the form of Andromeda.' Persinna feared that her black husband would not believe that the baby was his. So she decided to expose it. The infant was found and adopted by Charicles, a priest of Delphi. In due course she became herself a priestess of Artemis.

On the occasion of the Pythian Games at Delphi the Aenian delegation is headed by Theagenes, 'another Achilles', and it is Chariclea, in her capacity as priestess of Artemis, who has to hand him the torch to kindle the fire on the altar. Calasiris, an Egyptian priest of Isis, witnesses their meeting. He declares:

'We had the evidence of our own eyes that the soul is divine, having kinship with heaven. For as soon as they saw each other the two young people fell in love, as if each soul had recognised its like, at first sight, in the other and hastened to take possession of its perfect match.'

It is hardly necessary, perhaps, to draw attention to the Platonic source of this passage.

Theagenes competes in the race for men in full armour. He wins it and receives the palm from Chariclea. She consents to elope with him, but only on condition that he swears 'never to unite with her in the bonds of Aphrodite until she was restored to her rank and family or, if heaven denied her such restoration, at any rate until she consented with her whole heart to become his wife. Otherwise she would never be his.' Theagenes, himself a virgin, 'took the oath in the names of the Pythian Apollo, Artemis, Aphrodite and the Loves. He guaranteed to act in all respects as Chariclea wished.' We might say, in short, that he became the 'true knight' and slave of his lady. The lovers, in plighting their troth to remain chaste until marriage, were thus anticipating a certain type of chivalrous or 'courtly' convention.

In the course of their separate travels and adventures, which took them from Delphi to the Nile delta and then to Ethiopia, Theagenes and Chariclea met on several occasions. 'They then embraced as if they formed but a single being, abandoning themselves utterly to their ever chaste and virginal affection, mingling the warm floods of their tears and exchanging only the purest of kisses. When Chariclea perceived that the passion of Theagenes was growing somewhat over-intense, she restrained him, reminding him of the oath he had sworn. He then had no difficulty in controlling himself. He found it easy to exercise prudence. For, though love had enslaved him, he remained the master of his senses.'

This exemplary pair eventually found the happiness they deserved. But first they were subjected to ordeal after ordeal, each worse than the last. The jewels and the scarf embroidered with Ethiopian characters, with which Persinna had adorned her child before abandoning it, enabled the queen to recognise her daughter, when the latter was about to be sacrificed by the natives to their gods. Even Hydaspes acknowledged in the end that the white-skinned maiden was his own offspring. Theagenes also once more escaped death at the last moment. At length he married, to his delight, his beloved Chariclea. His gallantry, the sufferings he had endured and his patient chastity certainly entitled him to receive his reward.

A novel called *The Adventures of Leucippe and Clitophon* has come down to us under the name of Achilles Tatius of Alexandria. The date of composition is uncertain. It may be either prior or subsequent to that of the work of Heliodorus. Some passages at least seem to have been written later.

'Atmosphere' is created right from the start by a description of a picture in the temple of Astarte at Sidon. The painting showed Europa being carried off by Zeus in the form of a bull.

'All round the Bull dolphins and Loves, at their playful frolics, were depicted so vividly that they seemed to move. The Bull was following Eros, who had the features of quite a little boy, with outspread wings, a quiver and a lighted torch in his hand. He was looking back at Zeus and smiling, as if in mockery of the god who had for his sake turned himself into a bull. I was deeply impressed by the picture, for I had myself sworn eternal love. But I concentrated my gaze chiefly upon Eros as he drew the Bull along. "Well", I exclaimed. "Just look at that urchin! He rules the sky, the earth and the sea!"'

Clitophon, a Phoenician of Tyre, is supposed to be himself relating his love-story to the author. He had been about to marry his half-sister, born of the same father but a different mother. Such marriages were regarded as perfectly legitimate in ancient Hellas. But Leucippe, the daughter of Clitophon's uncle, suddenly arrives from Byzantium. He immediately falls in love with her.

'The moment I saw her I was lost, overwhelmed by every kind of emotion; admiration, amazement, fright, timidity and shameless desire.'

But in this case love at first sight was not immediately reciprocated, as it had been between Chaereas and Callirhoe,

Theagenes and Chariclea. Clitophon had to embark upon a long series of manoeuvres in order to attract the girl's attention and eventually her love.

Although this novel, like the rest, is devoted to the praise of feminine beauty and normal sexual relations, two pederasts, Clinias and Menelaus, make their appearance. They tell the stories of their 'special friendships', vigorously attack heterosexuality and take part in a debate along classical lines, comparing the two kinds of love.

The author frequently likens love to a religious initiation, introducing the novice to the 'mysteries of the god Eros'. Clitophon had presented himself from the beginning as 'one of the initiates of the god'. Clinias, in the course of a lesson in amorous technique, instructs him as follows:

'If you obtain a private interview with the girl, make it a rule to keep silence, as in entering upon the Mysteries. Approach her quietly and embrace her without uttering a word.'

At last Leucippe consents to elope with Clitophon, as Chariclea had with Theagenes. The lovers take ship at Beirut for Alexandria. But at once they are involved in the innumerable and incredible ordeals indispensable to this type of fiction, including storms, shipwreck, capture by bandits, apparent death and all the rest of it.

Eventually the pair are temporarily rescued and find themselves alone together in a private apartment. Clitophon wishes to take advantage of this respite to initiate Leucippe 'into the rites of Aphrodite'. But she immediately resists him. For Artemis has appeared to her in a dream, enjoining her to remain a virgin until after marriage. Clitophon has had a similar dream. He agrees to wait.

The lovers are then subjected to an apparently endless succession of new trials. Leucippe is believed dead after having miraculously escaped from a number of would-be seducers. Clitophon is pursued by an ardent lady from Ephesus, to whom he yields only once. The author's realism occasionally goes rather far. A certain Charmides intends to make Leucippe his mistress. But Clinias, in order to induce him to wait awhile, tells him: 'Yesterday she began to menstruate. So she can't have intercourse at present.'

At long last the series of improbable catastrophes of course comes to an end. Clitophon marries Leucippe, who not only still loves him but has actually succeeded in remaining a virgin in spite of all her terrifying adventures.

All this ancient Greek fiction has a peculiar interest and charm of its own. It certainly deserves more attention than it usually gets today. But Grimal's verdict that 'this boisterous and colourful world is profoundly convincing' seems to me to overshoot the mark. The extreme conventionality of the tales is beyond dispute. We may as well admit that they appear thoroughly insipid to a modern reader, except when flavoured with a certain degree of erotic pungency, as in *Daphnis and Chloe*. The taste of our time demands more highly spiced literary fare, or at any rate less monotony.

Yet generation after generation of antiquity was delighted by these long narratives. They were also highly popular with Europeans of the sixteenth, seventeenth and eighteenth centuries, when they were often imitated.

Their importance in the present connection is unquestionably justified by the conception of love which they express. For it was evidently not only in the works of such a philosopher as Plutarch that the mystical ideas of Plato on the subject were transferred from homosexual to heterosexual practices. Most of the novels referred to above bear witness to a more or less Platonic ideal of love. Sometimes, too, they seem to anticipate the 'courtly' conventions of chivalry.

Marriage is undoubtedly considered in these works to be the only condition upon which human love can last and develop in time. We can see from the foregoing chapters that such is the culmination of a long evolution in ancient Greek morality. But beyond the horizon of the temporal world the 'sister souls' of several of these pairs of lovers perceive, as they suffer the cruel ordeals brought upon them by their heroic fidelity to each other in betrothal or marriage, a heaven in which they will be united for ever. Love, however chaste it may be, must pass through the fires of misfortune before it can acquire its full value. In the end it is only recovered through loss. It is shown in all these novels to be both the most important element in any human life and the one force capable of defying and conquering death itself.

GENERAL VIEW

PIERRE LOUŸS, the author of *Aphrodite*, wrote a short story entitled *A New Pleasure* in which he imagined that the robust shade of an ancient Greek courtesan, Callisto, the daughter of Lamia, paid him a nocturnal visit. She is surprised to find that nothing really interesting has been invented during the last two thousand years, particularly in the various delights of love.

'Among the parchments of your museums,' she asks, 'is there one which imparts to you the tradition laid down by Rhodopis? Your historians may know all about the politics of Pericles and the generalship of Alexander. But have they reconstructed the science of Aspasia and Thais? Are they sure that the sepulchre in which the delicate dust of Phryne lies did not cover for ever the secret of a pleasure now lost?'

She proceeds to pass on to the narrator a substantial slice of the 'tradition' of the great courtesans of ancient Greece, not in words but in deeds. Then, when about to leave, she expresses disappointment at not being able to take with her the memory of a 'new thrill of pleasure'. The narrator offers her a cigarette. She smokes it with such delight that on departing she carries off a whole packet. We deduce that the only 'new pleasure' of modern times is tobacco.

There is no need to read this story in order to recognise the evident truth that love, being as old as humanity itself, assumes forms essentially similar at all times and in all countries. But it is legitimate to suppose that this eternal sentiment has been given various shades of significance among different peoples in different ages. We may reasonably ask, therefore, what special characteristics appear to define love as conceived in ancient Greece.

Of all such 'qualitative' divergences between the aspects of love in that civilisation and our own the most instantly conspicuous is the homosexual. Among women, apart from

Sappho, whose case is, however, doubtful, the sin of Gomorrha does not seem to have had many devotees. But the practice named after Sodom is in a very different category. The love which as a rule 'dares not speak its name' spoke it very loud and clear in ancient Greece, at any rate from the sixth to the fourth century B.C. The habits of the upper social strata in many Greek cities at that period were deeply influenced by pederasty.

The claim already made in antiquity that homosexuality constituted a useful check on the number of births, the increase of which would have entailed impoverishment, famines and wars, cannot be substantiated. The political decline and dissolution of ancient Greece was not due to any excess of population, but to its opposite, an insufficiency of citizens, and furthermore to the practices, sanctioned by custom and law, of abortion and the abandonment of new-born infants. These proceedings naturally kept down the population.

It is even more foolish to believe, as did Schopenhauer, that pederasty arises from an innate, irresistible inclination, corresponding with the aims of the 'genius of the race' and representing a strategic expedient resorted to by nature to prevent mankind dying out. In this way, he supposed, men too young or too old to engender healthy children could satisfy their sexual instincts 'on the side' without injury to the interests of the species, which such instincts nevertheless existed only to preserve! It would be a waste of time to trouble to refute such nonsense.

The truth is that pederasty is a vice encouraged by abnormal social conditions, such as life in military camps or purely masculine communities. Society was essentially masculine in the classical period of Greek civilisation, even outside Sparta. Homosexuality in fact develops wherever men and women live separate lives and differences in education and refinement between the sexes militate against normal sexual attraction. The more uncompromising such separation and diversity become, the more widespread homosexuality will be.

Its greatest extent coincided almost precisely with what is called the 'classic' period, from the sixth to the fourth century. In the political, literary and artistic fields this era saw the most brilliant and imposing achievements of the Greek genius. The question arises whether there is any connection between the development of homosexuality at this time and the 'classic' degree of perfection simultaneously attained.

I do not myself think so. In the first place pederasty only affected one section of society at all deeply. But even in this class of the rich and well born the example of Pericles proves that some Athenians remained immune to the temptation. Secondly, I feel that many poets and philosophers must have taken up inversion as a fashion or affectation, almost a form of snobbery, without always having a decided taste for it. And finally there is no evidence that homosexuality met with any general social approval.

We may cite a paragraph by H.-I. Marrou (*Histoire de l'Éducation dans l'Antiquité*, p. 55) in support of this view.

'The theory advanced by some writers that ancient Hellas constituted a paradise for inverts is an exaggeration. The very vocabulary of the language and the legislation in most of the cities are proofs that inversion never ceased to be regarded as an abnormal phenomenon.'

True enough. For the act of sodomy is denoted in Greek by words which also mean to defile or dishonour, as well as a shameful deed, infamous conduct or base behaviour. Contempt for the passive partner is even more marked, if possible. He is said to have submitted to shameful abominations. Furthermore, the violation of a youth was throughout Greece a criminal offence, while at Athens and even in many Dorian States the laws forbade any carnal relations whatever between grown men and youths. Only at Elis does homosexuality seem to have been legally admissible.

Alcibiades, after he has given an account, in Plato's *Symposium*, of how he 'tempted' Socrates, confesses that he is ashamed of his conduct (217 d). The Greeks never 'canonised' the physical act of sodomy. They always kept up the fiction of 'educational' pederasty, by definition a perfectly respectable practice. However hypocritical this convention may have been, it was at any rate one way of doing homage to virtue. The Hellenes managed to lend the cult of homosexuality an atmosphere of refinement which contrasts with the vulgarity prevalent in certain Roman circles. The latter had learnt from the Greeks what came to be called the 'noble mystery' of active and passive inversion. But, like other disciples who imitate the worst features of their masters, they confined themselves to coarse debauchery. The immorality of the 'brotherhood' and its protectors in the *Satyricon* of Petronius is nauseating in comparison with the relative discretion and reserve of the Greek outlook in this matter.

There is no point in asking whether, if pederasty had been practically unknown in Greek civilisation, the Greek achievement would have been less impressive or, on the contrary, even more dazzling. For the development of homosexuality only modified certain aspects, not the basis, of the culture of that people. As an outstanding example, we may consider the teaching of Plato, which has had so much influence on Christian doctrine and remains a living force today. José Ortega y Gasset observed that:

'It is impossible to say how deeply Platonic thought has penetrated the basic layers of modern Western civilisation. The most ordinary people in the West constantly make use of expressions and ideas which go back to Plato.'

But Plato's theory of love would retain precisely the same value for us if he had founded his argument on heterosexuality instead of its opposite. This point has been conclusively proved by Plutarch. In any case, it is surely erroneous to believe that homosexuality alone can be spiritually productive, for the very reason that it is physically sterile. It was Plutarch, again, who showed that love between man and woman is far more prolific in a spiritual sense than inverted love.

Nor, incidentally, can it be maintained that pederasty flourished in the golden age of Greece and was only formally rejected during the decadence under the Roman Empire. For it is in fact Homer who represents the first creative period of Greek literature. He was always considered by the Greeks themselves as the best of all poets. Yet no allusion to homosexuality can be found in his works. Nor can the view so long held of the Hellenistic and Alexandrine era as a period of decadence be accepted today. For it was in many fields, especially in scientific progress, a time of intense intellectual activity in which remarkable discoveries were made. Homosexuality was certainly not unknown in that age, as we have seen. But the tendency was by then far less prevalent than ordinary sexual feeling. Above all, it is clear from the current praise of feminine beauty and the sentiments inspired by it that from the fourth century onwards the general evolution of Greek society was directed towards normal erotic emotion.

It is a mistake, therefore, to claim that pederasty was continuously and profoundly associated with the development of the Greek genius, the forerunner of our own civilisation. So far from having been a condition of ancient Greek culture, homosexuality was undoubtedly merely a contingent and transitory accompaniment of the spirit of Hellas.

Love in ancient Greece, accordingly, was by no means limited to the inverted form of that sentiment. We may be grateful for the fact, since no nation has been more effectively inspired by female beauty and its power.

We may well compare the Greek situation in this respect with our own, in a society which, if not wholly Christian, is at least strongly influenced by Christian ideas.

In theory the contrast appears at first sight to be complete. Christianity sets a very high value on chastity and virginity.

But, as we have seen, in many of the Greek temples dedicated prostitution was encouraged and even organised as an institution pleasing to the gods. Nor did the Greeks recognise the concept of 'sin', of the 'forbidden fruit', which nowadays constitutes at the same time an obstacle to love and an aid to its further refinement. They considered sexual relations to be an absolutely natural, simple and normal phenomenon. Agamemnon, for example, swears in the *Iliad* that he has had no such intercourse with Briseis, 'as would nevertheless be normal between man and woman'. Plato's proposal in the *Republic* that the warrior class should hold women in common did not appear nearly so shocking and scandalous to his contemporaries as it does to ourselves, now that centuries of Christianity have rendered us somewhat more fastidious in this connection.

But on closer examination the differences do not seem to be so great as might have been expected. Many ancient Greeks were led by considerations of honour, dignity, self-respect and respect for others to practise chastity and decency, the *sophrosyne* which the Athenians required of their wives but which was also regarded as a masculine virtue. The importance of moral self-control, even of virginity, was not emphasised by religious doctrine. But it was inculcated by experience and by philosophers. Both Socrates and Epicurus felt habitual chastity to be one of the primary conditions of spiritual freedom and clear thinking.

The cults of Artemis and Athena, the two virgin goddesses, inspired the most fervent of their devotees to adopt a positively mystical view of virginity. Thus Hippolytus in the tragedy called after him will have nothing to do with Aricia or anyone like her. In this spirit also most of the heroes and heroines of the Greek novels swear to Artemis to remain virgins until they marry and yield to Aphrodite 'in marriage alone'.

The Hippolytus of Euripides is also a disciple of Orpheus, whose votaries, it appears, were generally believed to have renounced carnal pleasures. Such is one of the reasons why his image is found engraved on the walls of some of the Christian catacombs. But in pagan antiquity the Orphic sect was considered an eccentric body, sometimes including charlatans. It is certain that the masses of the people did not follow the example of these vagrant 'monks'.

Although some cults, such as that of Aphrodite, favoured prostitution, others insisted upon at least temporary chastity in their priests and priestesses. The Pythia at Delphi, so long as her prophetic functions lasted, had to abstain from relations with any male. The priest of the temple of Heracles Misogynist in Phocis was also obliged to renounce carnal associations of any kind during the period of his office, one year.

Christianity did unquestionably develop and refine the sense of bodily modesty. But it would be a mistake to suppose that it began with the Christians. The Fathers of the Church as a rule show little consideration for the pagans, whom they regularly denounce most vigorously. But both Clement of Alexandria and Theodoret, Bishop of Cyrrhus, paid homage, like Plutarch, to the admirable virtue of many ancient Greeks. Theodoret even goes so far, in his *Remedies for Hellenic Diseases*, as to illustrate it by pungent detail.

'Lysidice, for instance, it is said, always bathed in her shift, through excess of modesty. As for Philotera, whenever she entered the bath, she only uncovered her body gradually, as the water rose over it, raising her tunic by slow degrees. On emerging, she dressed with similar precautions. One of the admirers of Theano, the Pythagorean, once observed: "You have a beautiful arm!" She replied: "Yes, but it is not for all to see." On another occasion she was asked how soon after sexual intercourse a woman might attend the Thesmophoria'—a festival of Demeter for women only— 'The answer was: "At once, if the man was her husband. Never, if he were someone else."'

As regards marital relations in particular, the common absence of affection between husband and wife which we

noted in Periclean Athens might be thought to be mainly the
result of the contemporary development of homosexuality.
But the converse would really be true. It was because the
Athenians could make little intellectual or emotional contact
with their wives that they sought satisfaction in these respects
elsewhere, among youths or courtesans.

Only those, moreover, who completely ignore the social
history of the Christian West could suppose that this lack of
conjugal affection was entirely restricted to ancient Greece.
At many other periods and in many other countries marriage
has been and in some cases still is considered a matter of
convenience and personal advantage, a social contract in
which love between the parties, so far from being felt to be
requisite, is often judged undesirable.

In pagan Greece, as we have seen, Plutarch and the
novelists active in the Roman period were the first to
suggest a mystical basis of conjugal affection comparable
with that which Plato advanced for homosexual attraction.
But although the Christians had at their elbows the Gospels
and the writings of St. Paul, in which matrimony is accorded
heavenly status, Christian Europe had to wait even longer,
several centuries, before the religious character of married love,
sanctified by its formal sacrament, acquired full recognition.

The severance of marriage from love has been fairly
frequently presupposed in the Christian West. The tale of
Tristram and Yseult, which is, incidentally, full of memories
of antiquity, has been brilliantly interpreted by Denis de
Rougemont as 'the great European myth of adultery',
suggesting that the deepest kind of love, in which passion
predominates, is barely conceivable except outside and in
violation of the bonds of marriage.

Lucien Febvre (*Autour de l'Heptameron*, Gallimard, 1944,
p. 140) noted:

'In that ancient meadow set apart for the gambols of the
procreative instinct mankind eventually, by the exercise of
miraculous patience and feats of imagination, sowed the

seed, tended the growth and cherished the flower of love. It was an amazing achievement of subtle genius. But the moralists, in a fright, turned their backs upon it. . . . For centuries no serious and strenuous effort, worthy of humanity, was made to regulate in depth the relations between love and marriage.'

Even in the sixteenth century Montaigne had nothing new to propose on the subject. But he reflects the spirit of the age when he writes:

'In so prudent a bargain'—he means marriage—'there is little wantonness of appetite, dullness and bluntness rather . . . whatever may be said, none marries for his own sake alone, but equally or even more for the sake of a posterity, to found a family. . . . So it is a kind of incest to apply to so venerable and sacred a relation the exertion and excess of amorous licence. . . . A sound marriage, if such there be, declines the company and condition of love.'

Mme. du Deffand, again, in the eighteenth century, observes:

'A contented household may still be found among the lower sort. But among persons of quality I know not a single instance of reciprocal affection or faithfulness.'

Later still, the position had not changed. Alain Decaux (*Amours Second Empire*, Hachette, 1958, pp. 234-5), after describing the attitude to love of society under Napoleon III, concludes:

'It is more disquieting to find, not so much an immorality characteristic of one period, as a whole society which has practically erased love from its private preoccupations by subordinating it to money. No society is ever uniform. The historian of morals can only seek to establish its dominant traits. When he is told of happy couples and marriages for love, he is bound to reply that they are exceptions. They merely prove the unacknowledged rule that the aristocracy and upper middle class of the Second Empire had no place for love in their matrimonial affairs.'

In ancient Athens also it was probably only at the lowest social level that people married for love. But unfortunately there can be no certainty in the matter, for no Zola of the fifth century B.C. ever depicted love-relationships among the masses of that era.

We need not therefore be surprised if Athenians in the time of Pericles were usually indifferent to their wives. It would be more reasonable to be struck by the fact that such pagans as Antipater of Tarsus, Plutarch and the Greek novelists arrived on their own initiative at so truly religious and even mystical a conception of conjugal affection.

In conclusion, we may feel that it was neither the existence of homosexuality, nor the absence of a sense of sin, nor the current ideas of marriage, which gave love in ancient Greece, throughout its history, so special and enduring a character.

The sole specifically Greek and lasting trait we have found in this connection, equally evident in the works of Achilles Tatius and Heliodorus, Plato and Homer, is an acute and refined sensibility to both masculine and feminine beauty, regarded as a gift of the gods, both the most precious and the most dangerous they could bestow. Coupled with this sentiment is the notion, perhaps naïve in modern eyes, that physical beauty is necessarily accompanied by moral, that a noble frame must owe its existence to a noble soul. Even such an early production as the *Iliad* represents Achilles as the most handsome as well as the most generous and courageous of the Achaeans, while Thersites is the ugliest, as he is also the most envious and base among them.

Yet neither Paris nor Helen, though both were adorned by every grace that Aphrodite could confer, were models of virtue and magnanimity. Nevertheless, the Greeks of later ages deliberately ignored this suggestion by Homer, for it ran counter to their instinctive inclination.

We have often stressed this point. It recurs like a leading motive in the present study. The Greeks ardently admired bodily beauty. They were accordingly in a better position than many other peoples to produce great art. But they never ceased to confuse physical with moral beauty. Their very language is significant in this respect. For the word *kalos* means both handsome and noble-minded, while *aischros* covers both ugliness and baseness, as already noted in Chapter 1.

Philosophers like Plato and the Stoics accepted this ambiguity as self-evident. They never discuss it. Their inability to distinguish physical and moral orders of being was a permanent feature, not only of the thought of Greek intellectuals, but also of the outlook most usual among ordinary citizens.

It is highly probable that the ease with which they passed, as if it were the most natural thing in the world, from the contemplation of visible to that of invisible beauty suggested Plato's majestic theory of the ascending stages of love. So far as ideas are concerned, it is clear enough that his argument has dominated the entire development of European civilisation, except at a few isolated points, and that it constitutes the chief contribution of ancient Greece to what may be called the metaphysics of love.

In any case, Anders Nygren (*Eros et Agape*, Aubier, 1944), a modern Christian theologian, has felt bound to define the love of God, which he calls *agape*, by reference to and contrast with the *eros* of Plato.

The Platonic theory of love, I believe, could only have arisen in ancient Greece. In the last resort it is this conception, irrespective of its basis, which might just as well have been heterosexual as homosexual, that best stamps, in the eyes of posterity, the Greek ideal of love, simultaneously a burst of emotion in the whole being of the person concerned and an act of intellectual recognition, both perfecting the individual and intimating immortality.